American Civil War Cavalry

MICHAEL BLAKE

ALMARK PUBLISHING CO. LTD., LONDON

First published — January 1973

ISBN 0 85524 098 9 (hard cover edition)
ISBN 0 85524 099 7 (paper covered edition)

Printed in Great Britain by
Martins Press Ltd., London EC1R 0EN
for the publishers, Almark Publishing Co. Ltd.,
270 Burlington Road, New Malden, Surrey, KT3 4NL.

Introduction

As this book is intended as a complimentary volume to the already published work *American Civil War Infantry*, many basic details dealt with in the earlier book are not repeated here, more attention being paid to variations and information peculiar to Cavalry. Thus the reader will often be referred to the Infantry book for further details. In addition to the Cavalry, North and South, information on the Indian units raised by both sides is included. The various early machine-guns employed are also covered. This book is not intended as a guide to the strategy and tactics of the war, nor a military history of its course; it is purely a handbook of information about the men involved, what they wore and the equipment they fought with. The details given concentrate on those which will be of use to the modeller and wargamer and therefore those wishing for more information on the causes and courses of the war are refered to the bibliography at the back of the book. The Southern mounted troops started the war better equipped, with more skill and horses and higher morale than their counterpart in the North. The South was a natural rider's country, and the Rebel cavalry ran rings around the poorly equipped, trained and mounted Federals. However, as the war progressed so the training improved in the North and equipment and horses were replaced. In the South whilst the soldiers may also have improved with experience his equipment and horses were not so easily replaced. Thus slowly the Federal cavalry began to gain the upper hand, eventually reaching a marked superiority over the Southern horsemen. I should like once again to thank my good friend John Robertson of Dundee for his apparently inexhaustable fund of information; Mick Bowling for access to his collection for reference and illustrations, and for his encouragement and advice; and to my wife Paul for her patience.

CONTENTS

Chapter 1: Organization

AS with the infantry the organization of both North and South cavalry units showed marked similarities.

Union Cavalry

The Regiment

At the outbreak of war, the Regular U.S. Cavalry consisted of five regiments. These were the 1st and 2nd Regiments of Dragoons, 1st and 2nd Regiments of Cavalry, and the Regiment of Mounted Rifles.

A regiment was composed of five squadrons of two troops each. In 1861 when a third cavalry regiment was raised it was of six squadrons. Following this the regiments were re-numbered in sequence one to six, and all were made up of six squadrons, each of two troops, or companies as they were called, until 1881.

A company was at first 100 troopers strong with a Captain, 1st Lieutenant, 2nd Lieutenant and supernumerary Lieutenant. In 1863 this was changed to companies of 82–100 men and the supernumerary Lieutenant was dropped. The squadron organization was replaced by battalions, usually of four companies, when troops were detached for service elsewhere.

The Regiment was commanded by a Colonel, with a staff of a Lieutenant-Colonel, three Majors, an Adjutant, Quartermaster Commissary (usually Lieutenants) and a Surgeon and assistant. In addition the Regimental NCOs were a Sergeant-Major, Quartermaster Commissary Sergeant, Saddler Sergeant, Chief Farrier or Blacksmith, and two Hospital Stewards.

A company included a 1st Sergeant, Quartermaster-Sergeant, Commissary Sergeant, 5 Sergeants, 8 Corporals, 2 Teamsters, 2 Farriers, 1 Saddler, 1 Waggoner and 2 Musicians.

The strengths given are the theoretical strengths, seldom actually achieved, or maintained on campaign.

The Brigade

Brigades were normally formed from four to six regiments.

The Division

Union divisions usually had two or three brigades.

The Corps

Corps consisted of from two to three divisions. Early in the war the corps was an administrative unit only, the cavalry being used in small detachments, and its potential wasted. Eventually General Hooker organized the cavalry of the Army of the Potomac into a corp and used it as a mass striking force.

Movement

The rates of movement were: walk, four miles an hour; slow trot, six; manoeuvring trot, eight; alternate trot and walk, five; manoeuvring gallop, twelve; full extended gallop, sixteen miles per hour.

Cavalry on the march would occupy a considerable space. A troop of 96 men in column of fours would stretch to 95 yards long. Up to 35 miles per eight-hour day could be covered with ease, but this could be pushed to far greater distances, for example 80 miles in 27 hours. Troopers could and did sleep in the saddle on forced marches.

Formations

Troops usually manoeuvred in columns of fours, a small flexible formation, which could pass obstacles and deploy easily.

The charge was either made in two ranks, or in accordance with later manuals, a single rank. However, a charge could also be made in columns of fours or double columns of fours.

Despite popular belief a charge was not made over any and all ground. Wherever possible the ground was scouted first, and obstacles cleared. A charge delivered over rough ground, fences or hedges, would break the ranks of all but the best trained and mounted troops, and would have a worse effect on those delivering the charge than contact with the enemy!

Cavalry would fight dismounted when required, eg, to take and hold ground until the arrival of infantry; to cover gaps in a battle line, to cover a retreat, to force defended places or ground impractical for cavalry. Dismounted tactics were used extensively by General John H. Morgan on raids. Typical deployment in action is shown in the diagram below. The number fours and the Corporals in each troop acted as horse-holders in action, as sheltered as possible but near to the firing line.

The cavalry's role was primarily, and traditionally, that of scouting and flank protection for the main army. On outpost duty the idea was two-fold: to set up a flexible screen against infiltrating patrols, and watch and report on enemy

CAVALRY REGIMENT IN ACTION DISMOUNTED

This is a typical deployment for a cavalry regiment. A: Skirmishers in open order in advance of the main body. B: The horse holders, number fours, are at C, in as sheltered positions as possible by taking advantage of any natural obstacles, eg, trees, rocks, hollows in the ground, but always readily available for the dismounted troopers to mount up quickly. D: Mounted companies on one or both flanks.

5

movements. Half the patrols strength formed the grand guard. In front and to both flanks of this at a distance of some 500 yards were pickets and another 500 yards from these, single vedettes.

Patrols moved continually from grand guard to picket. Early in the morning patrols went at least two miles forward from the vedettes. Pickets and vedettes remained saddled and bridled ready for action. This type of duty was especially hard on men and horses. In addition, search and destroy operations were mounted in increased numbers, and used more and more troops as the war progressed.

Negro Units

As described in the companion work, American Civil War Infantry, the Union authorities were reluctant to raise negro units, but during the war a number of units were formed and served with distinction.

The organization and uniforms of the six negro cavalry units followed that of the regular cavalry regiments. The officers were all white, but NCOs were negro.

1st Regiment U.S. Coloured Cavalry

This regiment was raised on December 22, 1863, in Virginia and North Carolina. It served in the Department of Virginia and North Carolina and then joined 1st Brigade, 3rd Division, 18 Corps, Army of the James in June 1864. In May 1865 it moved to the Cavalry Brigade, 25 Corps, Department of Virginia and Department of Texas, mustered out February 1866.

2nd Regiment U.S. Coloured Cavalry

Raised in Virginia and North Caroline in December 1863, it served un-attached with the Department of Virginia and North Carolina until June 1864, then joined 2nd Brigade, 3rd Division, 18 Corps, Army of the James. In May 1865 it moved to 25 Corps Cavalry Brigade, Department of Virginia and Department of Texas. Mustered out February 1866.

3rd Regiment U.S. Coloured Cavalry

Organized in March 1864 from the 1st Missouri Cavalry, African Descent, it joined 1st Brigade, U.S. Coloured Troops, District of Vicksburg. In April 1864 it transferred to Winslows Cavalry Brigade, District of Vicksburg, and then moved to the District of West Tennessee in January 1865, serving with the Cavalry Division in 3rd Brigade and later 1st Brigade. Mustered out January 1866.

4th Regiment U.S. Coloured Cavalry

The unit was organized in April 1864 from the 1 Corps d' Afrique Cavalry, and served in Louisiana, joining the 1st Brigade, 2nd Division USCT in October 1864, until mustering out in March 1866.

5th and 6th Regiments U.S. Coloured Cavalry

Raised in Kentucky in October 1864, they served with the 1st Division, District of Kentucky, Department of Ohio (later Department of Arkansas) and mustered out March 1866.

By August 1863 an estimated 37,000 Negroes were serving in the Union Army, and some 180,000 had served by the close of the war. These troops formed the nucleus for the additional regular negro units authorized in July 1866, two of cavalry and four of infantry. These two cavalry units were the 9th and 10th U.S. Cavalry who won fame and glory, fighting the Indians on the Frontier, as the Buffalo Soldiers.

Confederate Cavalry

Unless otherwise stated the situation in the Confederate Army was the same as the details given for the Federal forces.

The Regiment

Theoretically, organization was ten companies or squadrons of 60–80 men, plus one Captain, one 1st Lieutenant, two 2nd Lieutenants, and including five Sergeants, four Corporals, one Farrier and one Blacksmith. The Regimental officers were a Colonel, Lieutenant-Colonel, Major and an Adjutant, with a Sergeant-Major and a Quartermaster-Sergeant. Rarely did the actual strengths match these.

The Brigade

Formed from four to six regiments.

The Division

Contained up to six brigades.

Formations

The information given under Union Formations again applies. Cavalry was used in every possible way, and met in all combinations from sabre fights between mounted units, to actions with both sides dismounted, and included combinations of both.

The rifled musket with which the infantry were armed meant that *en masse* they need have little fear of a cavalry sabre charge and, indeed, such charges were met with contempt.

In the west the type of attack preferred often consisted of a blast from a double-barrelled shotgun fired at a full gallop at close range, then closing with revolvers for the *mêlée*.

Chapter 2:
Cavalry Uniforms

UNION

Regulation—Enlisted Men

The Revised Regulations for the Army of the United States, 1861 set out in great detail the prescribed uniform, both dress and fatigue, for officers and enlisted men. However, these Regulations were rarely subscribed to in every detail, particularly later in the war. Shortages of materials and equipment, and the American soldiers' distaste for uniformity, saw to that.

The dress hat was the same as for infantry, the black felt brimmed hat variously known as 'Hardee', 'Kossuth' and 'Jeff Davis', with a yellow hatcord, and looped up on the right side with the eagle clip. The brass crossed sabre device of the cavalry was worn on the front. When issued the hat had the same black plume and eagle device to hold up the side as the infantry. These gaudy decorations were usually quickly discarded if the hat was worn in the field.

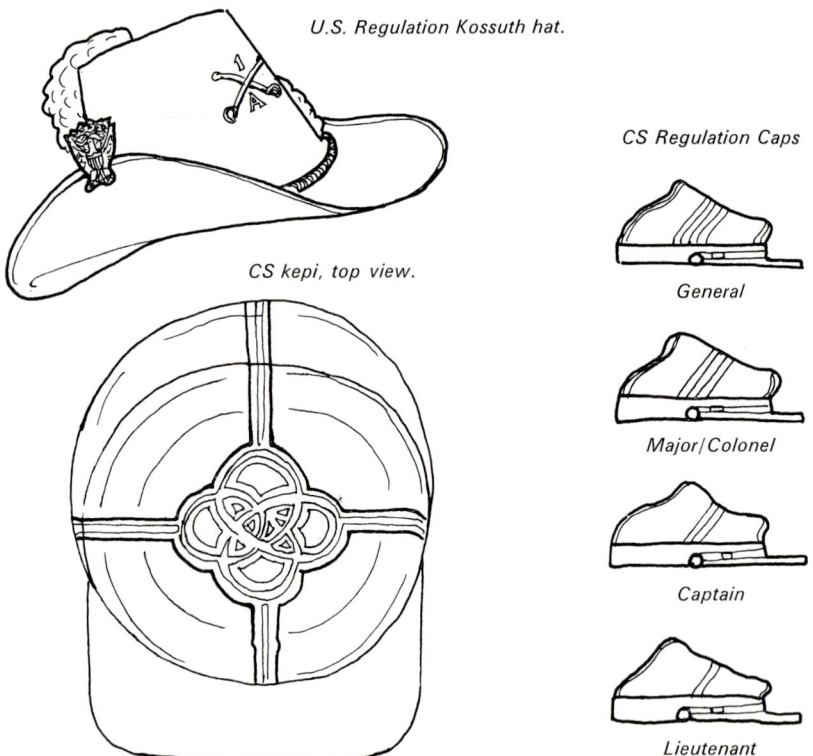

U.S. Regulation Kossuth hat.

CS Regulation Caps

General

Major/Colonel

CS kepi, top view.

Captain

Lieutenant

The shell jacket usually worn was short, reaching only to the waist, of dark blue cloth lined with white flannel. It had 12 small eagle buttons equally spaced down the front and two small buttons on the under-seam of the cuff. The stand-up collar was cut away at 30 degrees and had two blind buttonholes on each side in yellow worsted $\frac{3}{8}$-inch wide, each with one small button. The top buttonhole extended back 4 inches, the lower $3\frac{1}{2}$, and the top, bottom and front ends of the collar were edged with the same braid, as was also the front edge, bottom and the two back seams of the coat. The pointed cuff was formed from the same lace. To hold the heavy waist belt in place two small bolsters, piped in yellow, were attached to the back of the jacket. The jacket was often replaced by the issue fatigue blouse. This was essentially the same as the infantry's, a sack coat of dark blue flannel, reaching halfway down the thigh, loose, without lining. It had a falling collar, inside pocket on the left, and four buttons down the front.

The Regulation gave dark blue, but General Order No 108, December 1861, authorized sky blue for the trousers and very few men wore dark blue. The cut was loose, without pleats and made to spread well over the boot. However, as they were often worn inside the boot they were then made narrower, or a slit left along the side. They were also reinforced in the seat.

Regulations provided for either 'ankle' boots, ie, like modern low-sided shoes, or Jefferson boots, ie, higher lacing like modern work boots. However, troopers were more usually issued with a pair of riding boots. These varied from high jackboots, often the personal property of the owner and passed from father to son, to the smaller cavalry boot. Jackboots reached above the knee, but the cavalry boot reached just under the bend of the knee behind and arched higher, either in a curve or square shape, in front to cover the knee-cap. Another alternative was the equivalent to the modern riding boot, 14–17 inches high, cut level at the top just below the knee. All boots were full cut, to take the trousers when worn inside, and made of calf-skin or grain leather, black, with low flat leather heels and square toes. Inside the boots grey or neutral coloured socks, usually home knitted, and called stockings not socks. The army did, in fact, issue socks—four pairs a year. Sometimes gaiters or leggings of canvas, which buckled or buttoned at the side, were worn instead of the heavy boots.

Under the coat would be either the regulation grey shirt or a civilian one, or in summer probably nothing at all. Shirts of the period were all of the half-buttoned type, pulled over the head, and the collar little more than a fold-over of the material.

Over all this the cavalryman was issued a sky blue cloth overcoat, similar to that of the infantry. It had a stand-and-fall collar some 5 inches high, and double-breasted with two rows of large eagle buttons. The skirt was 6–8 inches below the knee, with a slit at the back for riding 15–17 inches long, which had a concealed flap and buttons for closing when required. The coat had a cape attached with hooks and eyes under the collar and reaching to the cuff, lined with yellow and had a single row of buttons down the front. It could be worn up over the head, thrown back over the shoulders or, as it was primarily intended, simply as additional protection for the chest and shoulders in foul weather. Also issued was a form of waterproof cape, called a talma, which had sleeves and reached to the knees. It was black and made from gutta-percha.

The brimmed hat was not popular with the troops, and was quickly abandoned in favour of the fatigue kepi or forage cap, exactly like that of the infantry, known later in the war as the 'bummers' cap. Both kepi and hat, under the battering of weather and wearer's fancy, were quickly contorted into an amazing variety of shapes.

All ranks were issued with fawn buckskin gauntlets with flared cuffs 6 inches or over long, often partially split to take the coat cuffs.

The eagle buttons had a C on the shield in place of the infantry I. The large brass shoulder scales were also to be worn but soon fell into disuse.

Non-Commissioned Officers

NCOs wore the same uniform as enlisted men, but with rank distinctions on the coat sleeves, halfway between elbow and shoulder, in yellow worsted lace.* The lace could be edged with black. The trouser seams were braided with $1\frac{1}{2}$-inch yellow worsted for Sergeants, $\frac{1}{2}$-inch wide for Corporals. A red worsted waist sash was issued to Sergeant-Majors, Quartermasters and 1st Sergeants for all duties except stable and fatigue, but was rarely seen except on parade.

Musicians

Trumpeters and Bandsmen had seven to nine rows of $\frac{3}{8}$-inch yellow worsted lace horizontally across the shell jacket, which according to Regulations should also be joined by vertical braid at the outer ends. The top and bottom bars were to be $6\frac{1}{2}$ inches long, expanding towards the centre of chest to reach the sleeve seams. The ends of the horizontal bars often had buttons, and the vertical braid might be omitted. Shortages as the war progressed meant that the braided jackets were usually reserved for parades, and plain jackets or blouses were worn on campaign.

Officers

The regulation coat was a dark blue frock coat, the skirts reaching from two-thirds to three-quarters down between hip and knee. This coat was single-breasted for Captains and Lieutenants, ie, Company Officers, and

*See 'American Civil War Infantry'.

RIGHT: CAVALRY JACKETS AND COATS
U.S. REGULATION SHELL JACKET (A)
The yellow (or orange on earlier issues) braid trim is clearly shown around the collar, cuffs, back seams, front and bottom of the jacket. The position of the collar braid can also be seen, and the two small belt bolsters which are also trimmed top and bottom with yellow braid.
VOLUNTEER SHELL JACKET (B)
The only real difference here is in the collar trim, with one braid and button only. The jacket is open at the front, a fashion which was widely adopted, both by Volunteers and Regulars, officers and men. The shirt or vest, of many patterns, colours and styles was exposed beneath—in the illustration the vest would probably have been red wool, and long-sleeved.
CONFEDERATE SHELL JACKETS
These are not illustrated as they followed the same basic pattern as those of the Union, except solid yellow collar and cuffs were called for, and the front and back seam trim omitted. The collar itself was usually smaller.
U.S. FATIGUE COAT (C)
This coat was usually plain, though some with yellow braid trim appear to have been worn.
OFFICER'S FATIGUE COAT (D)
This was of the same style as the men's but usually of a better quality material, with shoulder bars. The wearing of the belt inside the coat was widely adopted by men and officers on both sides.

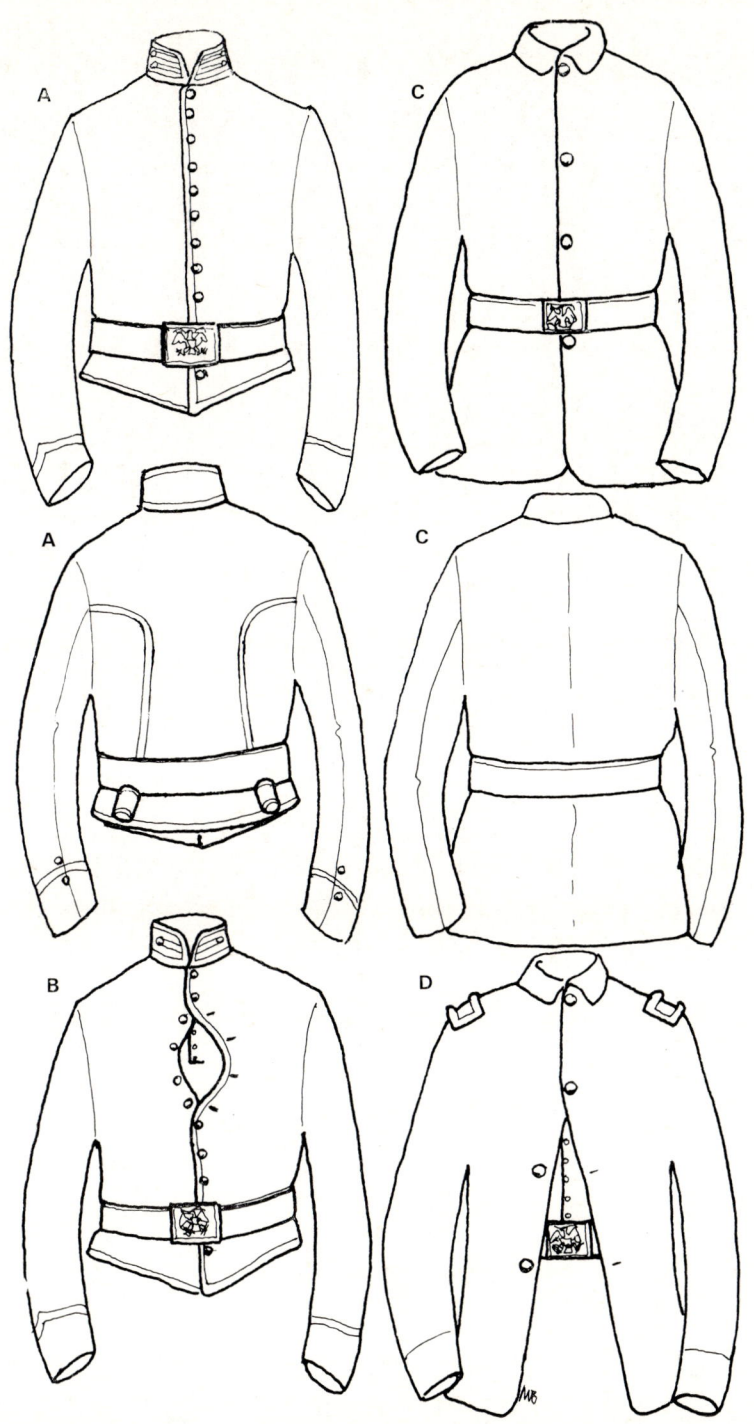

double-breasted for all other officers. Company Officers had nine buttons, Field Officers, ie, up to Colonel, two rows of seven buttons, and General Officers had buttons grouped to denote rank. Buttons were as for infantry.

This coat could be replaced by the dark blue short jacket or more usually the plain blouse without trim except for shoulder bars on campaign.

Generals and even other officers could, and did, design their own uniforms. General George Custer's wardrobe included a double-breasted black velvet suit with gold braid trim, with sailor collar over, CSA style sleeve braid, red neckerchief and brimmed hat. See Plate 2.

Trousers were sky blue for all officers, though as with other ranks dark blue was originally prescribed, except for Generals who did wear dark blue. The outer seams had $\frac{1}{8}$-inch yellow welt for all except general officers whose trousers were plain.

Hats were the same as the enlisted men's, but of better quality, the cavalry device being embroidered in gold on a gilt edged black velvet oval. The badges and devices differed with rank,† the cords being gold for Generals, who had three ostrich plumes, and all other officers had gold and black cords and two plumes.

All officers could wear vests, ie, waistcoats, the regulation issue being dark blue, white or buff. Overcoats were the same as for infantry officers.† Gauntlets were the same as the men's.

Rank insignia were the same as those worn by the infantry, in full dress epaulettes (see illustration on this page) and on active service shoulder bars or straps† with a yellow field up to Colonel.

† See 'American Civil War Infantry'.

U.S. FULL-DRESS EPAULETTES

A: *Shows a Lieutenant-General's epaulette, Other devices were two stars for Major-General, one star for Brigadier-General, an eagle for Colonel, an oakleaf for Lieutenant-Colonels, two bars for Captain, one bar for 1st Lieutenant, all silver on the gold epaulette. Majors had a gold oakleaf, and 2nd Lieutenants had a plain epaulette. (See Infantry for illustrations.) The gold bullion fringes were $3\frac{1}{2}$ inches long, $\frac{1}{2}$-inch diameter for all except Lieutenants, who had $2\frac{1}{2}$ inches, $\frac{1}{4}$-inch diameter.*

B: *Shows a 2nd Lieutenant's epaulette, with the regimental number worn by all regimental officers.*

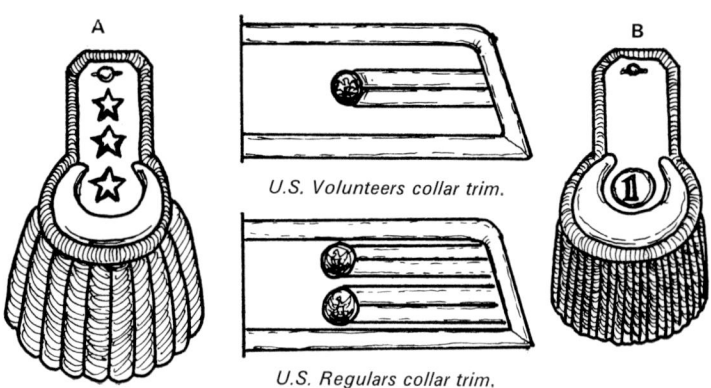

U.S. Volunteers collar trim.

U.S. Regulars collar trim.

U.S. CAVALRY OFFICERS AND BUGLER BOY

1. OFFICER, 3rd PENNSYLVANIA CAVALRY, 1862
This officer appears to have removed the collar and trim from the short cavalry jacket along with the shoulder bars. There is no sign of rank insignia at all, in fact. The hat was a light colour, possibly even straw from the shape. Trousers are regulation light blue without seam stripes. The checked shirt has a white collar attached, and a natty polka-dot bowtie completes the outfit. A watch-chain dangles at his waist.

2. OFFICER, 4th PENNSYLVANIA CAVALRY, 1862
A brimmed black hat (possibly the regulation Kossuth) has been battered into a style favoured by Major-General George Mead (see American Civil War Infantry, page 16). The frock-coat, even longer than prescribed, worn open to show the striped shirt and white collar. This officer has the shoulder bars to show his rank, and also wears gauntlets. Trousers appear to be regulation.

3. BUGLER BOY, PENNSYLVANIA CAVALRY, 1861
Based on a photograph of Jimmy Dugan, a bugler boy at Carlisle Barracks Cavalry Depot in 1861, who later served in action, the figure wears the regulation Kossuth hat with crossed sabre badge and plume. His jacket has no trim but the full-dress brass shoulder scales are worn. The trousers are the same dark shade as the jacket and, therefore, presumably dark not light blue.

4. OFFICER, U.S. CAVALRY, 1863
A variation on the regulation cavalry jacket with a fold-over collar and revers is worn by this officer, with trousers again the same dark shade as the jacket, and therefore dark blue. The shirt was pale, probably white, with a dark narrow bowtie. Again a watch-chain at the waist, and heavy gauntlets.

5. OFFICER, U.S. CAVALRY, 1863
A stiff, black, brimmed hat topped yet another variation on the U.S. cavalry uniform. The short jacket was regulation in cut but had Confederate style sleeve braid denoting rank, yellow trim around the collar and front edge, and was double-breasted. Trousers light blue with seam stripe, worn over the boots. Inside the jacket a white stand-up shirt collar is just visible.

U.S. CAVALRY OFFICERS AND TROOPER

6. MAJOR-GENERAL HUGH JUDSON KILPATRICK

As there are no rank insignia it is impossible to say if the uniform illustrated was worn by Kilpatrick when Major-General, or during his early career. It consists of uniformly dark (blue) jacket and trousers with (yellow) trim in the form of a simple loop on the sleeve cuff and around the edge of the cuff. Trim is also apparent around the bottom of the jacket and collar. The waistcoat is the same colour as the jacket and is also worn partly open. The shirt appears white. What appears to be the end of a waist sash can be seen hanging down behind the left hip but no sash is evident at the waist. Kilpatrick entered Union service in the 5th New York Volunteers (Duryeas Zouaves) as a Captain. On June 10, 1861, he was wounded at Big Bethel. He was made Lieutenant-Colonel of the 2nd New York Cavalry in September 1861, and took a very active part in the cavalry operations of the Army of the Potomac for the next two years. Constantly matched against Stuart's Cavalry in the Northern Virginia campaign, he commanded a brigade at Beverly Ford. He also took part in the Stonemans River engagement, destroying large quantities of Confederate stores and reaching within two miles of Richmond. In June 1863 he was promoted to Brigadier-General of Volunteers and commanded a cavalry division at Aldie, Middleburg and Upperville, Virginia. Brevetted Major in the Regular Army he took part in the cavalry assaults on the Confederate right at Round Top, Gettysburg. He led the Kilpatrick raid on Richmond and then transferred to command of the 3rd Cavalry Division in Northern Georgia for the Atlanta campaign. Wounded at Regaca, he was brevetted Colonel, and then served with Sherman in the invasion of the Carolinas, where his division did well. For his services in the capture of Fayetteville, North Carolina, he was brevetted Brigadier-General and then Major-General. He is credited with having coined the expression that 'cavalry can fight anywhere except at sea'.

7. COLONEL ALFRED DUFFIÉ, 1st RHODE ISLAND CAVALRY

This uniform is again based on the Regulations, the kepi being as prescribed. However the short jacket has very full sleeves and an unusual style of cuff trim. The collar and edges of the jacket are also trimmed (yellow). Light (blue) trousers tucked into long, black riding boots and white gloves complete the uniform. Colonel Duffié led the Federal left flank at Kelly's Ford when the Confederate forces were driven back.

8. TROOPER, U.S. CAVALRY VOLUNTEER REGIMENT

This is a hardy veteran later in the war when the Federal cavalry was a match for that of the Confederacy. The dark hat is a civilian one, but short yellow-trimmed cavalry jacket and light blue trousers are issue. The jacket, somewhat the worse for wear, is worn open, and the canteen is carried on the man instead of the horse.

9. OFFICER, 3rd PENNSYLVANIA CAVALRY, 1862

The kepi has no insignia, but shoulder bars indicate the officer's rank. The regulation fatigue coat is open at the throat with the shirt collar just visible above the dark (blue) waistcoat under the coat. The two straps across the chest are the belt support to the left hip and probably a binocular case on the right. The trousers are the same dark (blue) as the jacket.

NOTE: *All these sketches are baseed on photographs in Miller's 'Photographic History of the Civil War', which are, of course, black and white. Whilst they are of Union cavalry they show the great variation of dress worn (which was echoed by the enlisted men) throughout the war.*

CONFEDERATE CAVALRY IN THE WEST

These figures are taken from a photograph by Armstead & Carter in the 'Photographic History'. They show the variety of style and equipment, no two men having the same. There are 13 men with carbines and one with a sabre only (probably an NCO) and an officer. Of these all except one are wearing hats; three wear two straps, for carbine and canteen; seven wear one strap, for carbine only; three have no straps; at least three have revolvers thrust in their belts. They are all wearing trousers outside their boots except one, who has riding boots as shown in Plate 1. All the men carry sabres and carbines, except the NCO and officer who have sabres only. The clothing includes Union style fatigue coats, shirts and short jackets, worn buttoned and open. The officer's short jacket has large buttons and apparently Union style shoulder bars. Though lacking in gloss these cavalrymen did valiant service in Mississippi and Tennessee, and their fast and daring raids were a constant threat to Federal supplies. The trooper on the left has a captured Sharps carbine (the Confederate copy had no butt sideplate), whilst the cavalryman in the centre has a Richmond carbine. The trooper on the right, in addition to his two revolvers, has the favourite Confederate carbine, the Enfield Musketoon.

PLATE 1: UNION REGULARS

1. LIEUTENANT GENERAL 1861

This is the full dress uniform as prescribed in the regulations for Lieutenant and Major Generals. The dark blue frock coat has the buttons on the cuffs. In undress the uniform was the same, without the hat plume, waist sash and belt; the trousers would probably be worn inside high riding boots for mounted duty; the epaulettes would be replaced by shoulder bars. The collar and cuffs were to be dark blue velvet, but this was often omitted.

2. PRIVATE, 1st CAVALRY, FULL DRESS, 1861

Again the uniform is as per the regulations, and is the uniform in which the Union cavalry began the war. Prior to the 1861 reorganisation the two Dragoon regiments (which became the 1st and 2nd cavalry) had orange trim, whilst the two cavalry regiments (which became the 5th and 6th cavalry) wore yellow. The mounted rifles (3rd cavalry) had worn green. The brass shoulder scales, gloves, hat and plume, are the full dress items, and were rarely seen, even on parades, after the start of the war.

3. PRIVATE, VOLUNTEER CAVALRY, 1861-1865

This is how the typical Union cavalryman looked throughout the war. The insignia, until discarded, were worn on the top of the kepi because they were too big to attach to the front and still allow the flop-over style then in fashion. The heavy woollen four buttoned sack coat sometimes appeared in volunteer units with the cavalrys' yellow trim. The sabre would, of course, be carried from the waistbelt.

4. CAPTAIN, REGULAR CAVALRY, 1861-1865

The officer wears the same issue fatigue blouse as the volunteer private, with shoulder bars to indicate his rank. The light blue trousers have the yellow side seam stripe, and are worn inside the civilian riding boot. Again the sabre would be worn from the waistbelt. The coat was also worn over the waistbelt, see Fig D, page 10.

5. CORPORAL, IN REGULATION OVERCOAT, 1861-1865

The uniform underneath the overcoat could be that shown on either of the Privates, ie shell jacket, or the fatigue blouse. The carbine sling was worn over the coat but under the cape, which could be thrown back off the shoulders to facilitate use of the carbine and ammunition pouches if necessary. The waistbelt with the revolver holster and sabre were worn over the coat. The trousers have the NCO's yellow seam stripe; although this cavalryman is shown with them over the boots they could equally be tucked inside.

Plate 1 : Union Regulars

CONFEDERATE

Confederate Regulation

Just as elaborate Regulations were issued for the Confederate States as for the Union, but even less regard was paid to them. This was the result of the chronic supply problems in the South, which meant almost anything in the way of clothing had to serve as a uniform, and also because the Rebels refused to conform even with the Regulations of their own government.

Enlisted Men

The regulation coat was the same grey double-breasted tunic or frock as for the infantry, with all trim in yellow. The skirt extended to halfway between the hip and the knee; seven buttons in each row, the distance between the rows 4 inches at the top and 3 inches at the bottom; stand-up collar to rise no higher than would allow the head to turn freely, to hook in front at the bottom and slope back at 30 degrees on each side. The cuffs were $2\frac{1}{2}$ inches deep at the upper seam, to button with two small buttons, and slightly pointed on the upper part of the arm. Buttons had the regimental number or C, or even CSA, and were prescribed as $\frac{7}{8}$ inch and $\frac{1}{2}$ inch. The frock coat would rarely be found on anyone but officers, the men preferring the short shell jacket like that of the Federal cavalry, but with a smaller collar, again in cadet grey. The Regulations called for yellow collar, cuffs and the front and bottom edging trim on the frock coat. This might also appear on the shell jacket (but more often did not). Both might have any combination of yellow trim or plain grey trim, collar or cuffs, solid or braid.

Hats were not allowed for in the Regulations, the kepi being the prescribed headgear, but hats were, in fact, what nearly every trooper wore! They came in all colours and shapes, predominantly black, with and without ornamentation. The regulation kepi had yellow sides and crown and a dark blue band. All grey, and grey and yellow combinations, also appeared. The 1st Kentucky Cavalry Brigade appear to have worn an all-yellow kepi with otherwise regulation dress.

For fatigue duties a blouse, double-breasted, with two rows of seven buttons and small turnover collar, was listed in the Regulations, which was very similar to that described in a New Orleans newspaper in 1861 as the adopted regulation coat. No doubt some units were uniformed in this before the later Regulations of June 1861 were issued.

Trousers were to be light (or sky) blue cloth, loose and to spread well over the foot. The same alterations mentioned under Federal cavalry applied here too. The seat and insides of the legs were to be reinforced with canvas.

Boots were to be 'ankle' and Jefferson, but the details given for Union cavalry footwear applied equally well to the Confederates. During the first years of the war many items of clothing and equipment were taken from the Union troops in battle. This was whilst the Confederate cavalry was superior to its Northern foe, but as the balance swung the other way so the Rebels became less well equipped.

Butternut soon made its appearance amongst the greys and light blues, and in many cases replaced them entirely. This home-dyed clothing, both trousers and jackets, varied in final colour from khaki to reddish brown. Home-spun and tailored coats usually had slit or inserted pockets on sides and breast. Shirts were anything that could be obtained, often from Union sources.

Non-Commissioned Officers

The same uniform as the men was worn with rank chevrons on the sleeves and a $1\frac{1}{4}$-inch yellow seam stripe on the trousers, of cotton webbing or braid. Waist sash of worsted was to be yellow, but few were worn.

Overcoats of grey with stand-up collar, double-breasted, with cape to reach the cuff of the coat, with 18 buttons were prescribed, but contemporary reports say no more than two overcoats alike were ever seen!

Musicians

Buglers and Bandsmen were supposed to have the yellow frogging on the jacket but this was very rarely seen.

Officers

The Regulations called for the same uniform for regimental officers as for the men with appropriate rank distinctions on sleeves, collar and kepi. The trouser stripe was $1\frac{1}{4}$ inches wide yellow cloth. Waist sashes were yellow.

General officers had the same coat but with buttons in pairs and dark blue

PLATE 2: UNION VOLUNTEERS

The many volunteer regiments raised were usually uniformed and equipped like the regulars. However, many volunteer and especially militia units were given special uniforms when raised and these are illustrated in the colour plates,

1. GENERAL G. A. CUSTER

General custer wears one of his own distinctive outfits of a double-breasted black velvet suit, gold braid trim with a sailor collar over CSA style sleeve braid, a red neckerchief and brimmed hat.

2. 2nd U.S. CAVALRY, 1863

This Sergeant wears the old orange trim, which was originally the dragoon's colour until replaced by yellow, and also has the volunteer-style collar trim as on the 6th Pennsylvania, though this was a regular unit. It served in the 3rd Brigade, 1st Division Cavalry Corps, Army of the Potomac and Army of the Shenandoah.

3. 1st U.S. HUSSARS—3rd NEW JERSEY CAVALRY, 1861

Known, rather contemptuously, as the Butterflies, because of the hussar braiding on their jackets. The pill-box hat was probably replaced by the kepi later. The unit had a rather poor reputation, retreating hastily when fired on by Confederate artillery at Yellow Tavern. They served with the 1st Brigade, Army of the Potomac Division.

4. BENTON HUSSARS CAVALRY BATTALION, 1861

Their headgear was the old-style shako, which was undoubtedly replaced by the kepi as the war progressed. The colours are the regulation colours reversed, with the black hussar braiding on the jacket. Raised at St Louis, Missouri, late 1861, the unit served with the Army of the West and 1st Brigade, 2nd Division, Army of South-west Missouri up to February 1862 when it was incorporated in the 5th Missouri Cavalry Regiment.

5. 6th PENNSYLVANIA CAVALRY—RUSH'S LANCERS— 70th VOLUNTEERS, 1861

Raised by Colonel R. H. Rush from amongst prominent Philadelphians this unit wore the basic style cavalry uniform with the variation to the collar trim worn by volunteer units, in that there was a single centre braid instead of the regulars two. The trooper is shown in the earlier uniform with dark blue trousers. As the uniforms were replaced they would undoubtedly conform to the normal sky blue trousers. Enlisted men wore the crossed sabres on top of the kepi, officers on the front. A special plate, showing crossed lances, was worn on the carbine sling (see illustration on page 45). The men were originally armed with the 9-foot Norwegian fir lance with an 11-inch three-sided tip and scarlet swallow-tailed guidon. These were discarded in May 1863 and the regiment re-armed with sabres and carbines. The brass shoulder scales were also discarded later in the war. Their engagements included Antietam, Fredericksburg, Gettysburg, Brandy Station, Yellow Tavern and Cold Harbour, with the Army of the Potomac Cavalry Corps.

Plate 2: Union Volunteers

Plate 3: Confederate Regulars and Volunteers

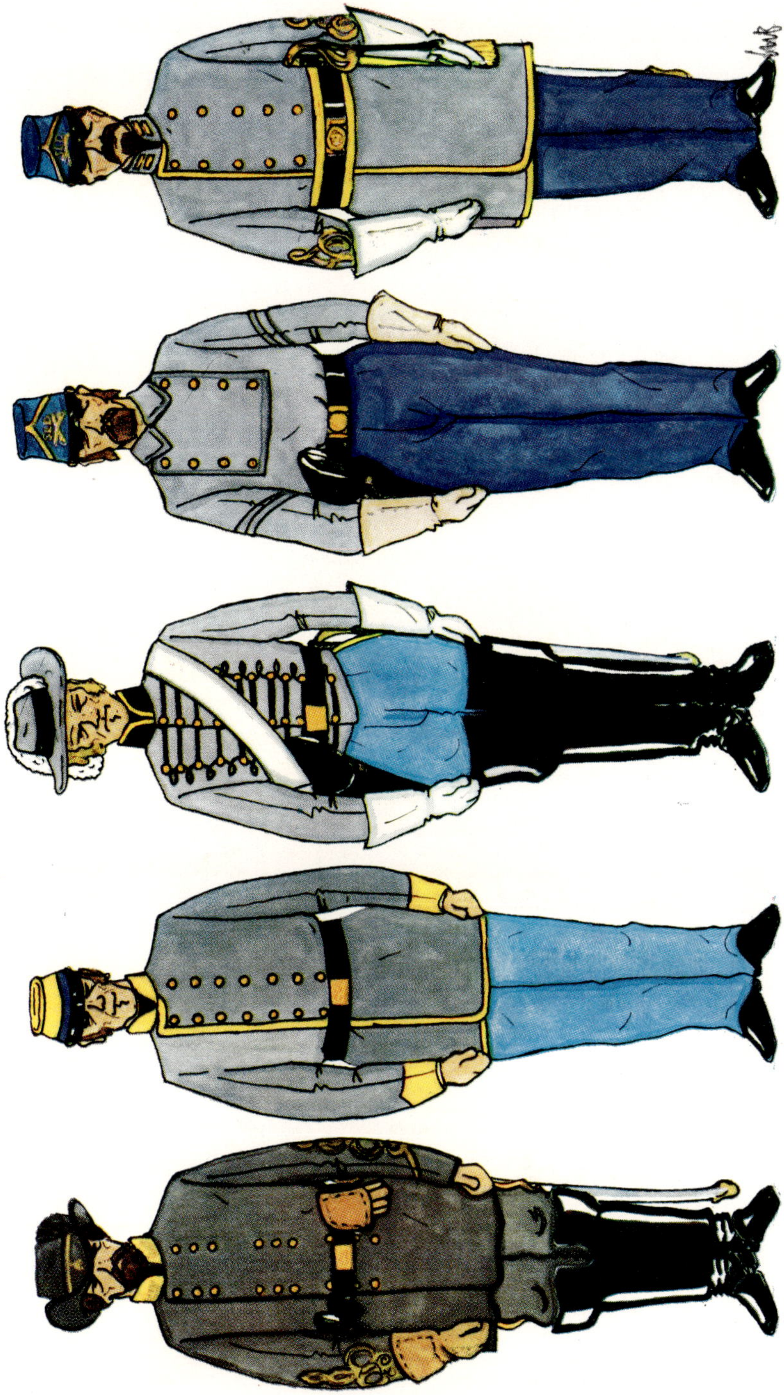

1 2 3 4 5

trousers with two gold lace stripes $\frac{5}{8}$-inch wide and $\frac{1}{8}$-inch apart. Waist sashes were buff silk net.

The coat was often worn with the fronts buttoned back, and apparently many officers had their coats lined with yellow thus making yellow facings to the coat). White or buff leather gauntlets like the Union officers were often worn. 1-inch and $\frac{1}{2}$-inch buttons were as for enlisted men, but as described in 'Infantry' for Generals, and staff.

The kepi decorations (see Fig 8) were one thin gold lace for Lieutenant, two for Captains, three for Majors and Colonels, and four for Generals.

PLATE 3: CONFEDERATE REGULARS AND VOLUNTEERS

1. CSA GENERAL OFFICER
This is the regulation style, but the colours are not, being all grey and of a darker shade than usual. The hat had a yellow cord and black plume. The frock coat has buttons in threes and a yellow collar but not yellow cuffs. The leather gauntlets were often tucked into the waistbelt when not being worn.

2. CSA REGULATION TROOPER
This is the uniform as called for in General Order No 9 issued by the Confederate States War Department in June, 1861, and seldom (if ever) seen, particularly on the enlisted men! The normal cavalry troopers equipment of carbine, sling, revolver in waist holster and sabre were, of course, all to be worn with this uniform.

3. GOVERNOR'S HORSE GUARDS, GEORGIA, 1861
This unit wore one of the many similar uniforms adopted by Confederate cavalry (the most famous being the 1st Virginia, see Plate 4, Fig 2) based on the hussar style. The braid is black, but the hat grey and plume white. The unit served in Company 'A' of Phillips' Legion (Georgia Volunteers) Cavalry Battalion, Hampton's Brigade.

4 & 5. SUSSEX LIGHT DRAGOONS, 'H' COMPANY, 13th VIRGINIA CAVALRY, 1861
The officers (5) wore a slightly longer version of the CSA Regulation frock coat, but with grey collar with rank device in gilt, and dark blue trousers. The trooper's (4) shirt had a buttoned plastron-type front which may have been reversible and yellow on the other side for full dress. The tall, dark blue kepi was almost a shako, with yellow braid and gilt 'SLD' over crossed sabres. The unit served in Imboden's Command.

CONFEDERATE PARTISAN RANGERS

1. BRIGADIER-GENERAL JOHN HUNT MORGAN

This sketch is based on a head and shoulders photograph of Morgan. The regulation frock-coat has the appropriate rank insignia on collar and cuffs, but is worn open in a relaxed manner. The trousers tucked inside the high boots were probably regulation light blue, but could have been grey or corduroy as on the officer in the coloured plate on page 21.

2. COLONEL JOHN SINGLETON MOSBY

Based on Mosby photographed with a group of his officers, this sketch shows the plumed hat so favoured by Confederate cavalry. The short grey jacket is without trim except the rank badge on the collar (which might be yellow). The trousers are very much lighter than the jacket, indeed they could almost be white. However, they were probably light grey or blue.

3. BRIGADIER-GENERAL TURNER ASHBY

Again based on a head and shoulders portrait, Ashby is shown wearing the frock-coat (which appears to be a rather dark grey in the photo) without yellow trim. The collar and cuffs are buff. The trousers are a blue-grey with two $\frac{5}{8}$-inch gold braids on the seam. The waist sash is buff silk with the general officers gold striped belt over it. According to the CSA Regulations the buttons on the coat should be in two rows of eight in groups of two, but these are seven (one under the sash) singly.

NOTE : These sketches illustrate not the actual uniforms worn by these officers but possibilities which they or any Confederate officer might have worn, based on contemporary descriptions.

Plate 4: Confederate Regulars and Volunteers

Plate 5: Confederate Volunteers

PLATE 4: CONFEDERATE REGULARS AND VOLUNTEERS

1. CHARLESTON LIGHT DRAGOONS—SOUTH CAROLINA VOLUNTEER MILITIA, 1860

This is, of course, the dress uniform and is particularly splendid, being almost Napoleonic in style. The plastron front was probably blue on the reverse. In December 1860 grey fatigue uniforms were obtained, and undoubtedly worn in action. The unit served as Company 'K' in the 4th Cavalry Regiment (Rutledge's Regiment), which was recruited entirely from Independent Volunteer Companies in South Carolina.

2. 1st VIRGINIA CAVALRY—BLACK HORSE CAVALRY, 1861

Undoubtedly the most famous of Confederate cavalry units, this one had a reputation for toughness. The uniform is again hussar style with black trim, though NCO rank chevrons appear to have been yellow. Black shoulder straps were not worn by all men. Certainly at the outbreak of the war the unit had all-black horses, but replacements were whatever could be obtained. Long hair in the cavalier style was favoured. Formed early in 1861 by Major J. E. B. Stuart it quickly reached ten companies and Jeb Stuart was made its Colonel. The unit served in Jeb and Fitz Hugh Lee's Brigades. 1st and 2nd Bull Run, Brandy Station, Yellow Tavern were amongst its actions.

3. 2nd CHEROKEE MOUNTED RIFLES—SERGEANT, 1861

As described in the text, the uniform was based on the Confederate regulations with individual Indian touches.

4. CSA CAVALRYMAN, 1862-1865

This trooper is clothed more or less in regulation fatigue jacket and trousers, though somewhat the worse for wear. The belts and equipment are brown leather, the red flannel vest is all that is worn under the jacket, and the kepi is a captured Yankee one! All very much in the Rebel cavalry tradition.

5. CSA OFFICER, 1862-1865

This illustrates one of the variations on the regulations described in the text.
The double breasted jacket has a yellow lining and is buttoned back to show this, rather in the style of 18th Century Uniforms. The breeches are buff coloured corduroy, a material greatly favoured by Southern cavalry officers. A binocular case hangs on one leather cross-strap, and the other is an additional belt support strap, to help with the weight of the sabre.

PLATE 5: CONFEDERATE VOLUNTEERS

1. HAMPTON'S LEGION—SOUTH CAROLINA VOLUNTEERS, 1861

Another hussar style was worn by one of the companies of this unit, this time trimmed in the cavalry colour. The red vest and black cravat with gold stick-pin was a personal touch, but the hat and plume were issued. The unit was raised by Colonel Wade Hampton as a legion of infantry, cavalry and artillery. The Beaufort Troop wore their own style uniform. This difference between companies and troops in the same regiment was common early in the war.

2. 1st TEXAS CAVALRY—HOOD'S OWN, 1861

The unit wore a variation on the CSA Regulation dress and, as with most Texan outfits, the 'Lone Star' device appeared somewhere, in this case on the buckle and probably buttons. Served in Fitz Hugh Lee's Brigade, the unit was also known as Texas Mounted Riflemen and Partisan Rangers.

3. 8th TEXAS CAVALRY—TERRY'S TEXAS RANGERS (1st REGIMENT TEXAS RANGERS), 1864

The many variations of Confederate uniforms are reflected in this unit. The hat could be black or grey; scarf yellow, pink or red; jacket grey, brown or blue, and it might have plain collar and cuffs or they might be scarlet; trousers grey, blue or brown, with or without the seam stripe. In fact, the unit generally wore civilian or captured Union clothing trimmed with scarlet. The unit was supposed to have had a smart uniform based on CSA Regulations, consisting of grey kepi with yellow base band; light grey shell jacket with yellow collar and cuffs; darker grey trousers with yellow seam stripe. But, as with most Confederate units, as the war progressed they had to make do with captured clothing.

4. 26th TEXAS CAVALRY—DEBRAY'S MOUNTED RIFLEMEN, 1861

The Confederate equivalent to Rush's Lancers, this unit was armed with the Mexican lance with blue over yellow swallow-tail pennant. Lancers were discarded in October 1862, Enfield rifles and revolvers being issued as more suitable for the trans-Mississippi theatre. Musicians wore the usual frogging on the jacket, but in green. The brass '26' appeared on the troopers and NCOs collars only. This was the proposed uniform, however, and it is not clear if it was in fact issued other than to Colonel DeBray and his Second-in-Command. The unit fought along the Rio Grande and in the Red River Campaign.

5. BEAUFORT DISTRICT TROOP, SOUTH CAROLINA, 1862

The hussar style all in grey, with the sombre black trim again in evidence. A troop of this name is recorded in Hampton's Legion, Company 'C'; 2nd South Carolina Cavalry Regiment, Company 'B'; and 3rd South Carolina Cavalry Regiment, Company 'C'.

LEFT: Union officer in greatcoat. His shabraque is of the 'trimmed' type with gold edging.

A

B

C

D

E

F

G

H

Plate 7: Confederate Flags

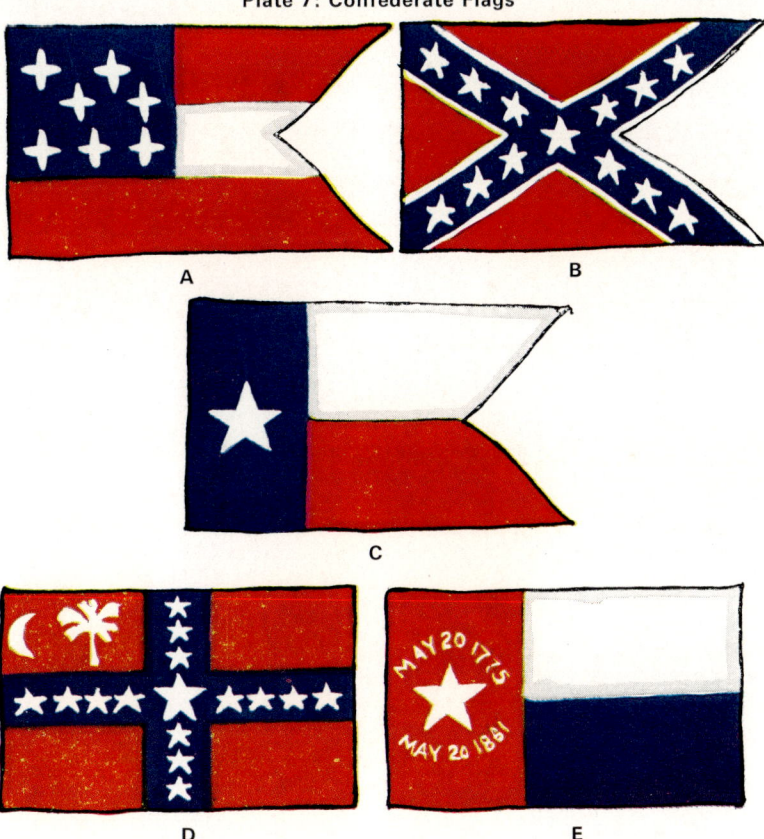

A

B

C

D

E

PLATE 6: FEDERAL CAVALRY STANDARDS, FLAGS AND GUIDONS
(Not to a common scale)

A: *Designating Flag, Headquarters, Cavalry Corps, Army of the Mississippi.*
B: *Designating Flag, Headquarters, Cavalry Corps, Army of the Potomac, 1864.*
C: *Cavalry Standard.*
D: *Designating Flag, Headquarters, Cavalry Corps, Army of the Cumberland.*
E: *Personal Flag, Major-General Philip H. Sheridan, Army of the Shenandoah and Cavalry Corps, Army of the Potomac, 1864–65.*
F: *Designating Flag, Reserve (3rd) Brigade, 1st Division, Army of the Shenandoah.*
G: *Company Guidon, 1863–65.*
H: *Company Guidon prior to 1863 and after 1865.*

PLATE 7: CONFEDERATE FLAGS
(Not to a common scale)

A: Stars and Bars Guidon
This guidon was based on the 1st National, but had seven four-pointed stars in rows instead of the normal five-pointed stars in a circle. The regulation design was also used for guidons.
B: Battle Flag Guidon
C: Texan Cavalry Guidon
D: South Carolina Regimental Colour, 1860–61
E: North Carolina State Colour
This is a variation on the basic North Carolina design which is the present State flag, having a blue canton with the lower date of April 12 1776, both dates on gold scrolls, 'N' one side of the star and 'C' the other; and a red bar over a white bar. On the flag illustrated the lower date is that of the State's secession from the Union.

Chapter 3: Equipment

Union Enlisted Men and Non-Commissioned Officers' Personal Equipment

The trooper and NCOs wore a heavy 3-inch wide black leather carbine sling about 60 inches long across the left shoulder. The sling buckled at the back with a large brass two-tongued buckle at one end and a brass belt tip held in place with rivets at the other. To hold the carbine on the belt, sliding loosely, was a three-piece swivel consisting of a loop and polished steel snap hook, which attached to a carrying ring or bar set in the left side of the carbine in the small of the stock. The buckle was usually worn at the back, and the carbine hung down at the right hip. To help overcome the problem of having the carbine hanging loosely against the horse and man, when mounted, a carbine socket was provided for in the Regulations. This was a waisted cylinder of black leather $2\frac{1}{2}$ inches high and $2\frac{3}{4}$ inches in diameter, with a buckle and strap attached to the quarter strap on the right side of the saddle. The muzzle of the carbine was pushed into this socket when mounted to hold the carbine steady. The waist belt was also black leather, which adjusted to size by folding back to the right through a slot in the belt plate, with a single sharp brass hook fitting into one of the holes in the belt. A brass catch on the left end of the belt engaged in a flat blunt hook on the back of the plate to fasten the belt on. The buckle was covered by the heavy brass lead-filled rectangular eagle belt plate like the infantry officers'. The two sabre slings were attached separately to the belt by brass rings on stitched-on straps, a short sling at the front at the centre of the hip, and a longer sling 7–8 inches round to the rear. Joining the brass rings of the belt, just above the slings, an additional strap could be worn. This was narrower than the belt and adjusted at the back with a single hook, passed over the right shoulder and hooked with a heavy brass hook onto a large brass ring on the left hip, and was intended as extra support for the sabre.

On the waist belt a smaller version of the infantry cartridge box was worn; flatter and with a single tin inside, usually at the rear of the hip. This was for carbine ammunition. A second box of the same type was worn on the other hip to hold revolver ammunition. At the front was a cap pouch like that of the infantry for percussion caps, again one for the carbine, one for the revolver. The trooper might reduce this bulky load by carrying the caps and cartridges mixed, or by using combination pouches. A brass oval 'US' plate was worn on the cartridge box.

Spurs were, of course, issued to all mounted troops. The regulation spurs were brass, with loops for the leather straps which passed over and under the

U.S. button.

Carbine swivel hook.

CS button.

foot. The spurs had goosenecked up-curved shanks and small sharp-toothed steel rowels, which could cut a horse badly if misused. The spurs could be, and were, modified to make neck spur rather than strap spurs. The strap slots were cut off, the edges rounded and three small holes bored in the spur, at the ends and below the rowel shank. Small nails were then used to nail the spur to the boot heel.

Musicians
Buglers did not carry the carbine or sling. The bugle was brass with a yellow cord.

Officers
Belts and buckles were as carried by Infantry Officers.

Confederate Equipment
The proposed standard equipment for the Confederate trooper was essentially the same as his Union foe. However, supply difficulties usually meant that the equipment carried was widely different in materials if not in design. Often the regulations were met from captured Federal supplies. Leather was more usually natural brown than black, black dyes being in short supply in the South. The cartridge pouch would probably have 'CS' or 'CSA' stamped in the leather rather than as a separate plate, and the cap pouch might well be treated the same way. Cartridge boxes, cap boxes and belts were also frequently made from prepared cotton cloth, with three or four thicknesses stitched together to save on leather. Buckles were the same as for the Infantry.

Musicians
As with the Federals, no carbine sling.

Officers
As for Infantry Officers.

Union Enlisted Men and Non-Commissioned Officers' Horse Furniture
The most important piece of equipment was, of course, the saddle. This was

LEFT: Union Cavalryman from an old print showing from left to right: a cavalryman in overcoat; cavalryman mounted in undress order with brass shoulder scale, carbine sling and cartridge box, elaborate shabraque; cavalry officer showing rear view; cavalry corporal in parade dress. The hat is held up at the left side and the carbine buckle is shown on the chest, both in contradiction to most sources.

RIGHT: Confederate Cavalry from an old print showing from left to right: cavalry general with white plume in hat; cavalryman in almost regulation dress except for kepi. Trousers are dark blue which is unusual. Note method of carrying sabre hilt forward strapped under saddle holsters and girth strap. Also the carbine is on a strap over the back rather than on the usual sling and hook; cavalryman in slouch hat in place of kepi and again dark blue trousers; Infantryman is on extreme right.

CONFEDERATE AND UNION CAVALRYMEN

Left to right: Rebel trumpeter in civilian coat with a neckerchief at his throat; Confederate officer in greatcoat; Confederate officer in normal uniform jacket; Federal cavalry officer on foot with sabre in the 'hooked-up position'; probably Confederate cavalryman with U.S. style stirrup covers, and again is wearing a neckerchief; figure in foreground is a Rebel with a slung rifle, wooden canteen and a tin mug hanging from the saddle rear; another CS officer with what could be a fatigue coat.

U.S. CAVALRY: CORPORAL, VOLUNTEER REGIMENT

This Corporal wears the regulation uniform, but has trousers with elastic tapes passing under the instep to keep the trousers down, and the volunteer type collar trim. The position of the equipment on the horse is apparent. At the front, over the pommel, is the rolled greatcoat; at the rear the saddle bag is just visible under the blanket and tarpaulin, which has a tin mug on one strap. The orange stripe is clearly shown, as are also the webbing girth and surcingle.

the regulation McClellan saddle, designed by General George B. McClellan, which replaced the old Army Ringold type. It was of wood with an open slot down the centre over the horse's backbone with two side bars fitted flat against the horse, which were joined by a fairly high wishbone pommel at the front and a rounded cantle at the rear. The whole frame was covered with shrunken rawhide with sewn seams along the edges of the side bars. Unfortunately the rawhide tended to split and crack through exposure to the elements, which was rough on the rider! The saddle came in three sizes, 11-inch, 11½-inch, 12-inch seats, a plate riveted to the pommel giving the size.

CS CAVALRY: TROOPER

Wearing very near regulation uniform, this trooper carries however a double-barrelled shotgun on a webbing strap, and a straight 'Prussian' style imported heavy cavalry sabre. The holster is also probably one of a pair. On the horse is a canvas sack over the pommel under a greatcoat (possibly a captured Yankee one;), a plain blanket under a Confederate adaption of the M1842 Grimsley saddle with high cantle and pommel, and at the rear a canteen and rolled blanket.

Fastened to the side bars by brass screws were two saddle skirts, heavy black leather aprons hanging to around midway down the sides of the horse on either side. Girth or quarter straps of heavy leather ran diagonally from cantle and pommel to the central girth strap rings. The girth passed from these rings under the horse's belly, and was of heavy blue webbing $4\frac{1}{2}$ inches wide. Over the saddle and horse went the surcingle as a kind of safety strap, again blue webbing, $3\frac{1}{4}$ inches wide and 60 inches long, with a tongue buckle and leather ends. The leather stirrup straps, attached to the side bars just behind the pommel, passed under and out through slits in the saddle skirts. Attached to them were triangular leather fenders or sweat leathers which protected the legs from the saddle skirts, and at the ends wooden leather hooded stirrups. The stirrup straps adjusted with a buckle to the correct military seat, which had the rider seated on his backside in the saddle, stirrups shortened so that the foot rested level with the stirrup. The stirrups had a 3–4-inch tread, made from one piece of bent wood separated at the top by a small wooden bar or transom around which the stirrup leathers looped. Stirrup hoods were heavy leather riveted to the wooden frame covering the whole front and sides and extending $2\frac{1}{2}$ inches in front of the tread to take the toe, and often stamped with 'US'.

At the front and rear of the two side bars were stapled four brass rings intended for crupper, breastplate and martingdale, but more often used for sabre or canteen when the other non-essentials were discarded on campaign. The martingdale, sometimes combined with the breastplate, was intended to make the horse keep his head down. It attached by strap and ring to the bridle or reins and thence to the cinch, saddle or breast strap. The breast strap itself was a strap around the horse's neck, two ends fastening on the front rings on the saddle, the other end to the cinch under the horse. Occasionally a brass insignia was attached at the joint of the strap. The crupper served the same purpose at the rear, and consisted of a padded ring which the horse's tail passed through, with straps to the rings on the saddle. Breast straps were useful in heavy going by taking some strain off the girth, and were worn by some volunteer units.

Under the saddle the regulation blanket was folded as a pad. It was 67 inches by 75 inches, and was folded first along its length, then twice more the other way. The blanket was dark blue wool with an orange border stripe and 'US' in orange letters in the centre. Some grey blankets with yellow trim were used.

Strapped over the pommel with three long straps, through slits in the saddle, was the rolled overcoat or talma. On the cantle behind the rider went the blanket and tarpaulin, again rolled and held by straps. Over a stud on the back of the cantle went the leather flap joining the two saddle bags, leather bags 14 inches by 15 inches. In these went curry-comb and brush (which were also sometimes carried in smaller pommel bags at the front) with clothing, rations, extra ammunition, spare horseshoes and nails, and a 14-inch iron picket pin for grazing the horse. The iron curry-comb, 'Carpenter's No 333 Pattern', had a wooden handle and three double rows of teeth, whilst the leather-backed brush fitted flat in the palm with a strap which fitted over the hand. A 30-foot lariat was coiled and hung from a saddle ring or the halter. An empty nosebag for the horse was carried tucked over one end of the rolled blanket on the cantle. The cylindrical canvas bag had straps to go over the horse's nose and fasten round its neck.

The black leather halter of cheek pieces, noseband and large hitching strap ring for use in tieing the horse had no bit. A watering bridle with reins and simple snaffle bit could be attached to the halter. The black leather riding bridle, worn over the halter, consisted of cheek straps down the sides of the head to the bit rings at each corner of the mouth; a crownpiece passing over the head behind the ears; a browband going across the forehead above the eyes; throat latch billets or straps which went round the neck; and occasionally a noseband just above the bit, passing from cheek strap to cheek strap.

The Army Model 1860 blued steel bit was issued in four sizes. No 1 was called the Spanish bit, with a hump or port of $2\frac{1}{4}$ inches and a curb ring, and was for horse-breaking; No 2, with a 2-inch hump and curb chain; No 3 with a $1\frac{1}{2}$-inch port; and No 4 with a $\frac{1}{2}$-inch port and curb chain. All bits were $4\frac{1}{2}$ inches between branches or cheeks, which were S-shaped, the reins

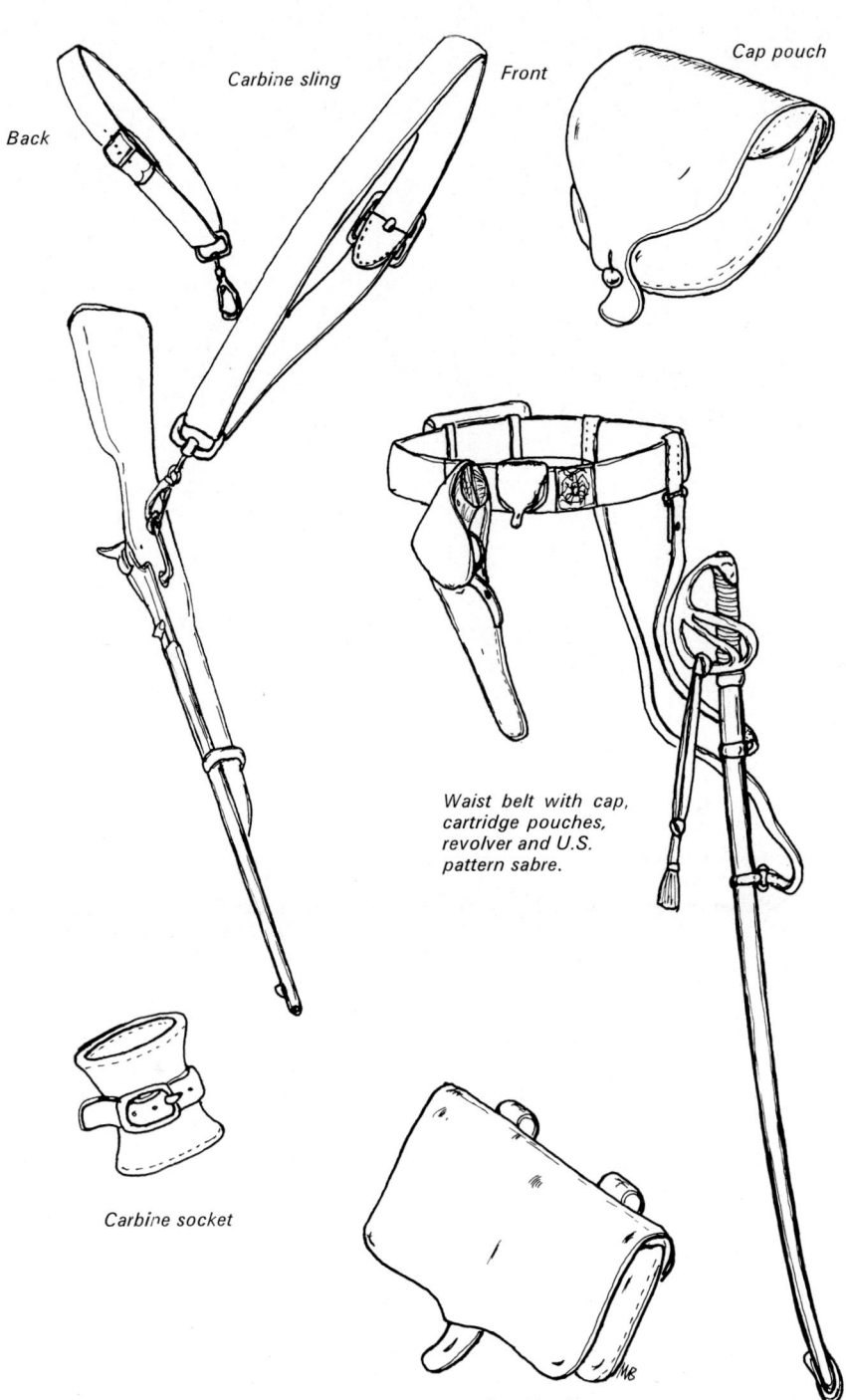

Back

Carbine sling

Front

Cap pouch

Waist belt with cap,
cartridge pouches,
revolver and U.S.
pattern sabre.

Carbine socket

Cartridge box

37

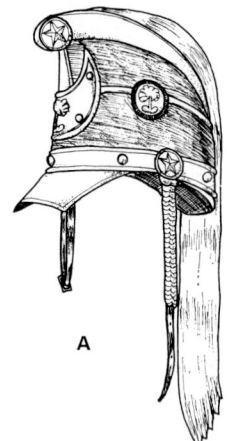

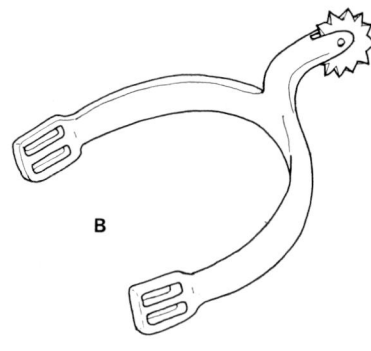

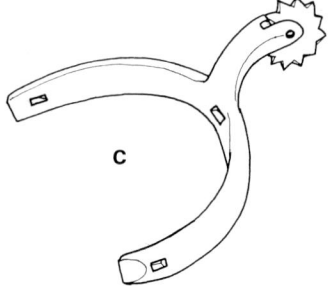

A: Charleston Light Dragoon Helmet
The helmet itself is black with brass or gilt fittings, including the peak and chin strap decorations. The State emblem, a Palmetto tree, appears on the helmet, and the crescent plate at the front may well have been designed to repeat the crescent moon which appeared on the South Carolina flag. The horse-hair plume was white. **B: Regulation Spur (U.S.) C: Modified Spur**

attaching to rings at the bottoms, held apart by a crossbar. The curb chain, or ring, went under the jaw to provide leverage for the bit in the horse's mouth, and in the Model 1863 bit fastened to hooks below the eyes of the side branches. On either side where the branches joined the mouthpiece were brass bosses, stamped 'US' or sometimes with the regimental number or company letter. 2½-inch brass 'US' or 'USA' rosettes were worn above and behind each eye to hold the browband and throatlatch in place.

The reins were 5 feet long with the ends sewn together, attached to the curb bit. When the troopers were in action dismounted, to enable the horse-holders to hold a number of horses, a 15-inch link strap buckled onto the left rein ring on the bit, with the strap of the other end hooked into the bit of the next horse. When not in use this hooked onto the throatlatch buckle. A picket line, a long rope to hitch the horse when in camp, was also carried.

Officers

Officers used the McClellan saddle, but often non-regulation outfits were used. Flat or English saddles were often used, as were Grimsley and Jennifers or artillery-type saddles, General U. S. Grant favouring this type.

Over the saddle officers were supposed to wear the shabraque, dark blue, with a 1-inch gold edging lace as for mounted Infantry Officers. Underhousings, ie, the straps, were also blue.

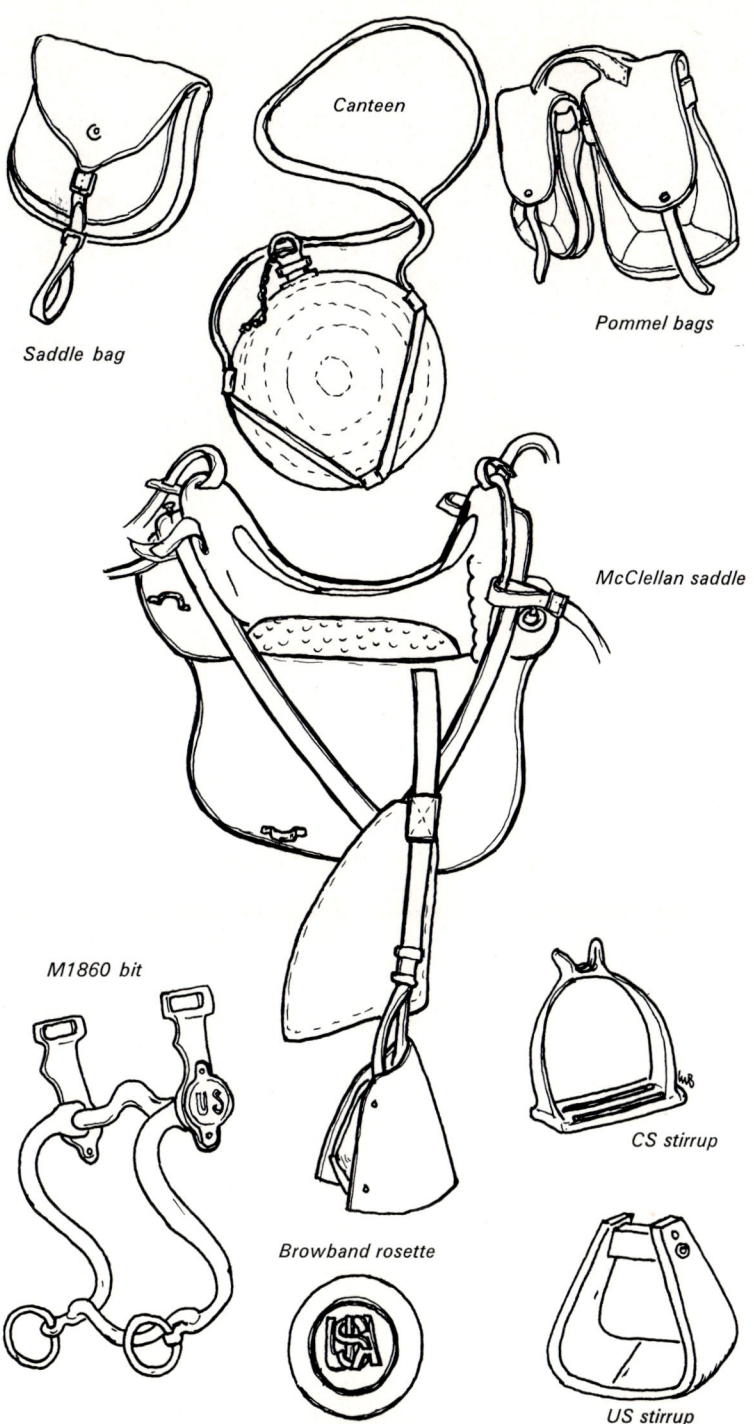

Canteen

Saddle bag

Pommel bags

McClellan saddle

M1860 bit

CS stirrup

Browband rosette

US stirrup

39

Officers also had a black leather valise bag, 16 inches long and 5–6 inches in diameter, worn like a blanket roll. Generals often had a more elaborate type, and also had saddle holsters.

Officers usually had double reins, with one pair to a snaffle or bridoon bit, the other to a curb bit. The rosettes on the bridle were sometimes of the eagle type, and Generals had stars.

Horses

The original recruiting regulations required troopers to supply their own horses and equipment, but this was later changed so that the trooper was entirely equipped by the government. This applied in both regular and volunteer units, and included remounts.

Confederate Enlisted Men and Non-Commissioned Officers' Horse Furniture

Again much of what has been said about the Federal equipment applies to that of the Confederate Cavalry also, particularly as much was captured from the Union forces early in the war. Many militia units had good equipment, but the volunteers often had civilian saddles and equipment, at least until their first clash with Union forces. Cavalry saddles came last on the Confederacys list of priorities for leather, after cartridge boxes and artillery harnesses.

Jennifer tree-type saddles were adopted, especially as J. E. B. Stuart favoured this type, along with the older Grimsley. Unfortunately both types rode down on the horse's backbone and withers if the condition of the horse was poor, causing sores. The McClellan was eventually copied by Confederate manufacturers, and many imported saddles were also used. Heavy cast brass stirrups were used rather than wooden ones.

A large number of U.S. Dragoon Model 1842 and 1850 bits were used, these having been issued to the militia units before the war, as well as imported ones.

Usually Confederate equipment was much simpler than that of the North, rope being used for leather, halters discarded, saddle bags replaced by canvas bags or haversacks, even small plain sacks. Blankets varied, anything available being used. Bosses and rosettes were more likely to be plain brass, but CS and CSA stamped types were used.

Officers

As for enlisted men, even officers, equipment was, especially later in the war, much simpler than the Union officers, even to plain blankets, ie, no shabraques or lace trim.

Horses

The Confederate system called for the cavalryman to supply his own mount, for which he was paid *per diem* for the use and if the horse was killed in action. However, if the horse died for any other reason, even the hardships of the campaign, the trooper had to find and pay for his own replacement. This might well mean that the cavalryman had to transfer to the infantry if he could not find a mount, and many valuable veterans were lost to the cavalry because of this.

Chapter 4:

Cavalry Flags and Badges

Union Flags: Standards

Each regular regiment carried only one standard, the Regimental Flag. This was dark blue, 2 feet 5 inches on the fly, 2 feet 3 inches on the lance, fringed with yellow, on a 9-foot lance. The eagle was in natural colours, ie, brown wings and body, white head, neck and tail, and beak yellow; shield blue over red and white stripes; scrolls red with gold lettering 'E Pluribus Unam' above, the regimental number, eg, 'Second U.S. Cavalry' below; the 13 stars white; leaves green with red berries; 10 arrows white. The standard of the 2nd Dragoons had over 25 stars.

Union Flags: Guidons

Companies also had a swallow-tailed guidon, by 1861 Regulations divided in half, red over white. On the red, 'U.S.' in white, and on the white the company letter in red. In 1863, however, the guidon was changed to a Stars and Stripes in the same swallow-tailed style. This was again changed in 1865 back to the original style. The guidons were 3 feet 5 inches from the end of the tails to the pole, 15 inches from the centre of the fork, and 2 feet 3 inches on the pole, which was again 9 foot.

Regimental standard bearers were usually Sergeants, guidon bearers Privates. The butt of the lance was carried in a socket on a special right stirrup. Dismounted, the lance was carried in the bend of the right arm, vertically, with the butt approximately 1 foot from the ground. The flag bearer followed the unit commander unless otherwise ordered. The lance head was heart shaped and plain.

Standards and guidons had a real purpose during the Civil War, acting as rallying and leading points in the confusion of battle.

Union Flags: Personal Flags

Personal flags were used by some individuals to indicate their location on the field regardless of the actual position they held. Generals Sheridan, Merritt, Kilpatrick and Custer all carried personal flags. Major-General Philip H. Sheridan's was probably the most famous, though by no means the most colourful. General Custer had four different personal flags at various times throughout the war, two of which are illustrated. The first flag was a simpler version of the second without the fringe and with only the battle honours Boonsboro and Falling-Water. The third flag was a simpler and smaller version of the fourth without the white cord edging.

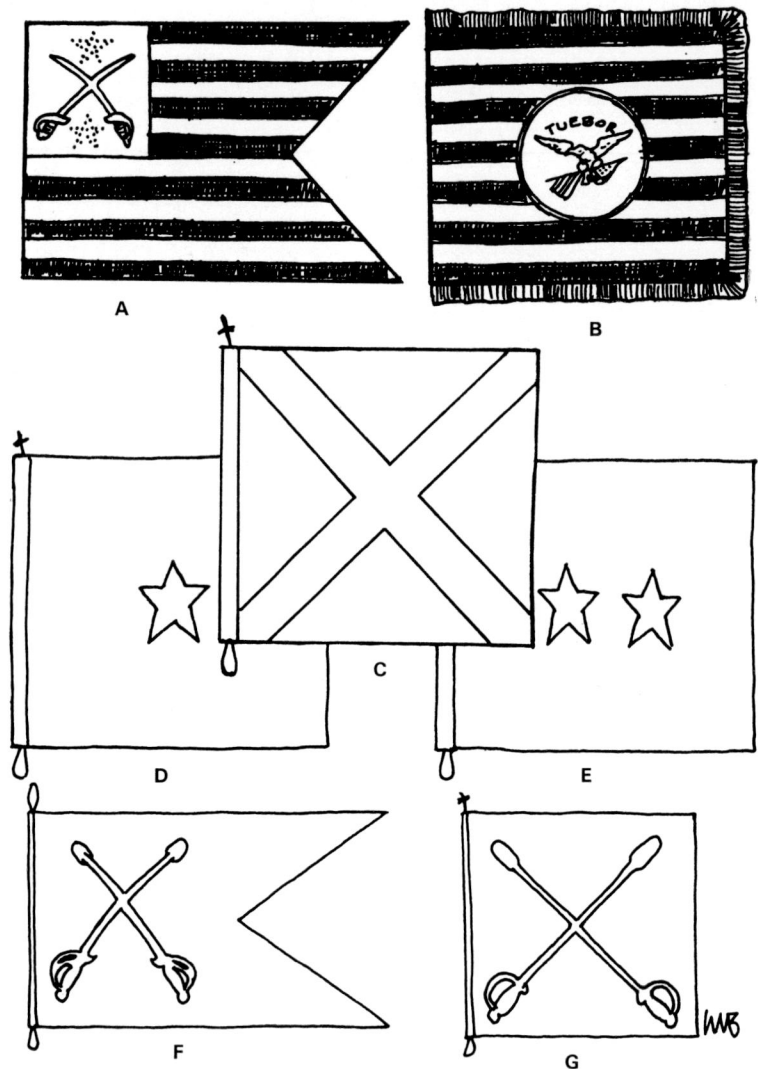

FEDERAL PERSONAL AND DESIGNATING FLAGS

A: **Personal Flag, Brigadier-General Wesley Merritt, 1st Division, Cavalry Corps, Army of the Shenandoah and Army of the Potomac, 1864–65.** *Silk field of red and white stripes, sky blue canton with embroidered gold sabres, and 36 silver stars arranged to form two five-pointed stars.*

B: **Personal Flag, Brigadier-General Hugh Judson Kilpatrick, 3rd Division, Cavalry Corps, Army of the Potomac, 1864.** *Silk, red and white stripes, gold fringe, red central disc bordered white with eagle and stars and stripes in natural colours.*

C: **Designating Flag, Cavalry Reserve Headquarters, Army of the Potomac, 1862.** *Yellow field with blue cross.*

D and E: **Designating Flags, 1st and 2nd Cavalry Brigades, Army of the Potomac, 1862.** *Yellow fields and blue stars.*

F: **Designating Flag, Cavalry Corps Headquarters, Army of the Potomac, 1863.** *Yellow field with white sabres.*

G: **Designating Flag, Cavalry Reserve Brigade, 1st Division, 1863.** *Blue field with yellow sabres.*

Union Flags: Designating Flags

In order to show the location of the headquarters of a unit, designating flags were prescribed by the Regulations, in similar styles to those for the infantry.

Corps Flags

General Order 53 of May 12, 1862, provided for designating flags for the Headquarters of the Cavalry Corps of the Army of the Potomac. In 1864 Sheridan introduced a new Cavalry Corps flag. Headquarters of the Cavalry Corps of other armies appear to have adopted flags at various times (see Plate 6).

Division Flags

Sheridan also designed Divisional Headquarters flags in 1864 for the Army of the Potomac Cavalry Corps' three Cavalry Divisions, similar to his own personal flag and the Company guidon. In 1865, following Circular No 31 a rectangular Divisional Headquarters flag similar to those in use by the infantry (see Plate 6 and illustrations on opposite page) was adopted instead of Sheridans's design.

Brigade Flags

Supplemental orders to General Order 102 of March 24, 1862, provided for flags for the Headquarters and the two brigades of the Cavalry Reserve, Army of the Potomac. General Order No 53 of May 12, 1863, described the infantry brigade flags, and Circular No 31 called for similar designating flags for the cavalry brigades. There appears to have been some delay in the issuing of these flags as some other forms of brigade flags were used (see Plate 7 and illustrations opposite and on page 44).

Cords and Tassels

The Regulations specified the cords and tassels for infantry and artillery regiments, but no similar details appear to have been issued for the cavalry. This did not mean that cavalry commanders did not use them on their flags, presumably they did but to their own design.

OVERLEAF: FEDERAL CAVALRY PERSONAL AND DESIGNATING FLAGS
T: **2nd Personal Flag, General G. A. Custer, October 1863–June 1864, 2nd (Michigan) Brigade, 3rd Division, Army of the Potomac.** *Red over blue silk field; painted sabres with silver blades, brass hilts, brown handles; battle honours gilt, shaded below and to the left in black; gilt fringe. 52 inches on the fly by 35 inches on the pole.*
U: **Designating Flag, Headquarters 3rd Division, Cavalry Corps, Army of the Potomac, 1865.** *White field with blue sabres.*
V, W, X: **Designating Flags, Headquarters 1st, 2nd and 3rd (Reserve) Brigades, 3rd Division, Cavalry Corps, Army of the Potomac, 1865.** *White fields with red sabres, blue bar and border.*
Y: **Designating Flag, Headquarters 3rd Division, Cavalry Corps, Army of the Potomac.** *Red over white bars, numerals reversed colours. Typical of the Divisional HQ Flags in use in 1864, the number of the Division appearing on the flag (see also colour plate 6). 72 inches staff to tips, 36 inches on the pole.*
Z: **4th Personal Flag, General G. A. Custer, March 1865–May 1865.** *Red over blue silk bars, with white crossed sabres and white cord border. 78 inches staff to tips, 36 inches on the pole.*
(Not to a common scale)

43

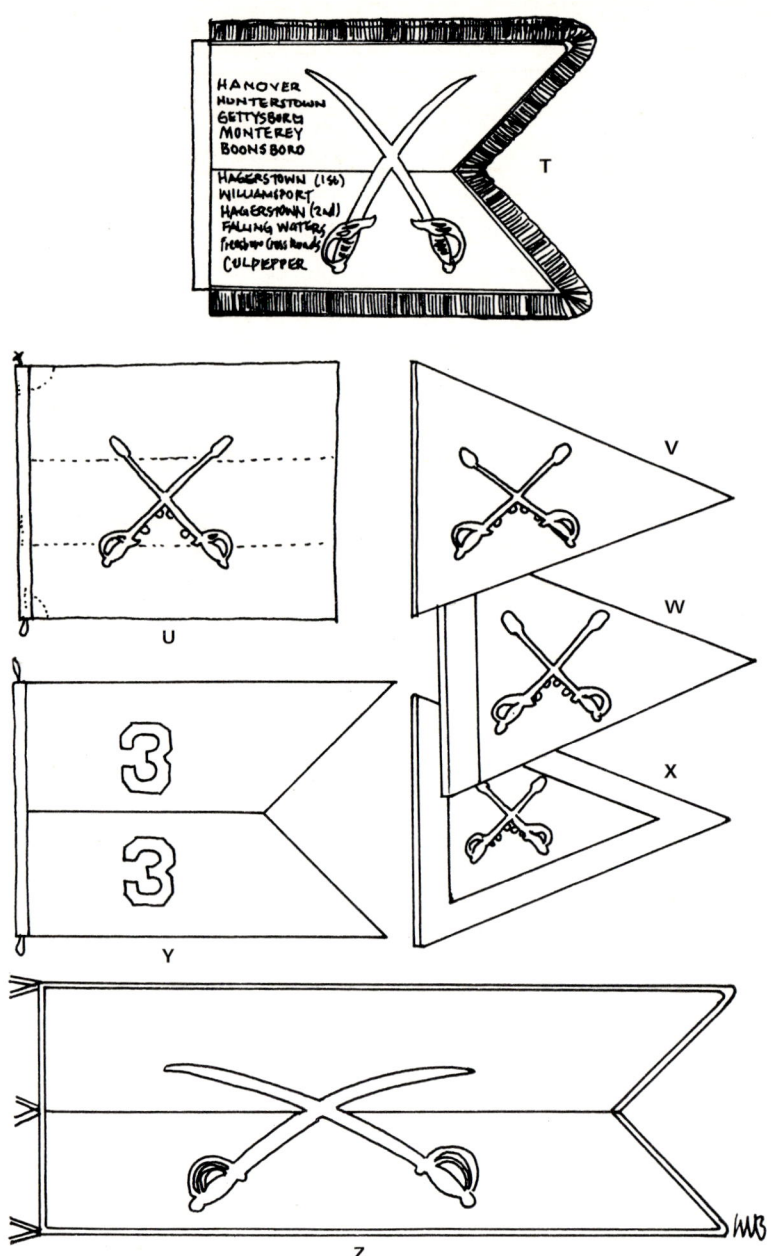

HANOVER
HUNTERSTOWN
GETTYSBURG
MONTEREY
BOONSBORO

HAGERSTOWN (1st)
WILLIAMSPORT
HAGERSTOWN (2nd)
FALLING WATERS
Freeriage Cross Roads
CULPEPPER

T

U

V

W

X

Y

3

3

Z

Confederate Flags

The Regulations called for one flag to be carried, but as with the Infantry the Regulations were largely ignored. The Battle Flag was around 30 inches square for cavalry, but also appeared in guidon form about the same size as the Federal guidon. The various National colours as described for the Infantry were also carried, together with all their possible variations. One guidon based on the Stars and Bars (Plate 7) had seven white four-pointed stars in a blue canton and red over white over red bars.

The Texan State Flag was carried in normal rectangular and guidon form. Many other flags were also carried by cavalry units, including the variations tried before a final National Flag design was accepted. Before the design shown in Infantry was adopted, South Carolina had a more complex design similar to the Battle Flag. This had a red field with dark blue St George's Cross with white stars, three in each vertical arm, four in each horizontal arm, with a

UNION INSIGNIA (not to common scale)

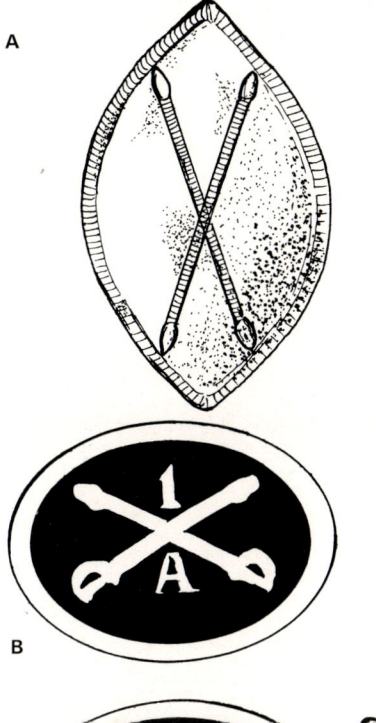

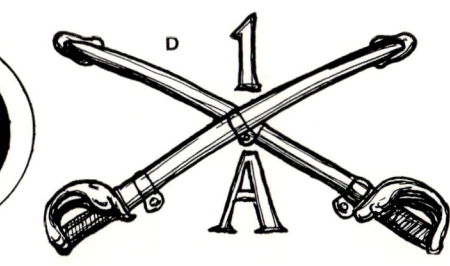

A: **Rush's Lancers (6th Pennsylvania Cavalry) Carbine Belt Plate**
This plate is very rare, and has the appearance of being rather crudely hand-stamped. The crossed lances refer, of course, to the Regiment's origins when it was armed with lances.

B: **Company Officer's Hat Badge**
Embroidered on black velvet, the edge and sabres were gold, the regimental number and company letter silver. The whole badge was a little smaller than the enlisted man's brass device.

C: **Regimental Officer's Hat Badge**
Details as for Company Officer's badge, but without the company letter.

D: **Enlisted Man's Hat Badge**
Stamped from sheet brass, all three emblems were sewn to the hat or forage cap using wire loops soldered to the backs. The company letter was 1-inch high, the regimental number $\frac{5}{8}$ inch, and the crossed sabres $3\frac{1}{2}$ inches wide by 2 inches high. The Regulations only called for all these on the brimmed hat; on the kepi only the regimental number was prescribed, but more often than not all three were worn.

45

large white cross in the centre. In the top left canton a crescent moon and palmetto tree in white. Some Arkansas units carried Battle Flags with a plain white cross on a blue field.

Union Badges

The Corps Badges described in the Infantry volume were not worn by the cavalry but two units had special badges of their own, worn on the hat or kepi.

Sheridan's Cavalry Corps had a white (probably silver for officers) sunburst with squared ends to the rays and a dark blue oval centre with crossed sabres in yellow or gold. Wilson's Cavalry Corps had a gold carbine with a red swallow-tailed guidon hanging points down from a tasselled gold cord; on the guidon gold crossed sabres (see illustration on the front cover).

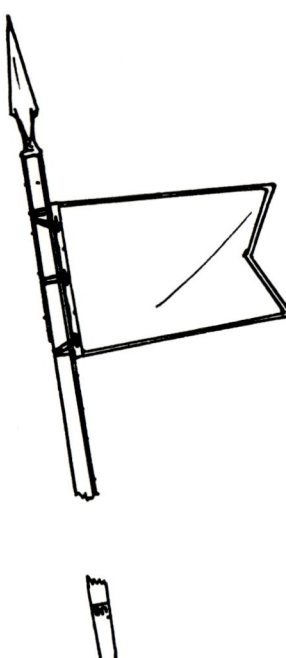

LANCE AND PENNON: RUSH'S LANCERS

This is the pennon and lance carried by the Trooper in Plate 2. The pennon, supposedly made by the ladies of Philadelphia for the regiment, was of deep crimson bunting, swallow-tailed and tapered along its length. The pennon was 11 inches wide on the hoist (ie, against the staff), 16½ inches from points to hoist and 12½ inches from swallow cut to hoist. Three edges were bound with ¼-inch scarlet piping like that used as trim on artillery jackets. The fourth, hoist edge had a narrow piece of scarlet cloth with three buttonholes, which the single scarlet cord tied the pennon to the lance. The lance itself consisted of a steel point 8⅛ inches long which was attached to a brass ferrule, 4 inches long, ending in a knurled brass ring; the wooden shaft and a tapered brass counter-poise 5⅝ inches long. The latter was held on by a single counter-sunk screw, and was stamped 'U.S.' The point was fixed to the shaft by two ¼-inch wide brass straps, one 9⅛ inches long and the other 37⅞ inches long. These had three and nine brass screws respectively. The ferrule was stamped 'U.S.' and 'U.S.P.'

A and B: Sharps 'Coffee Mill' Carbine M1859
This unusual weapon had a 'Coffee Mill' mechanism replacing the brass patch box. View A shows the detachable crank handle, and the hole (arrowed) into which the coffee beans were poured. View B shows the other side of the butt, the ground coffee coming out of the slot in the round central plate. It was proposed that one of these guns be issued to each company, but few in fact saw service.

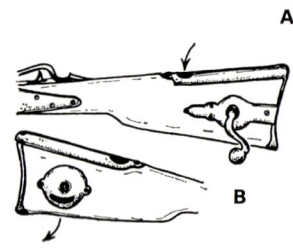

Chapter 5: Weapons

Union

The Regular and Volunteer regiments were armed along similar lines. Each trooper was armed with a sabre and revolver (as soon as supplies permitted) and at least two squadrons in each regiment were armed with carbines or rifles. Later all cavalry regiments were equipped with single-shot carbines for all troopers. Officers carried the revolver and sabre only.

Sabres

Initially the sabre was of the long, straight Prussian pattern, but this was replaced by a light cavalry sabre with 36-inch blade, the Model 1850. This had a brass three-barred guard with black leather wire wrapped grip and a black leather, 1 inch by 18 inches, doubled sword-knot which ended in a long leather tassel and was fastened to the guard and looped around the wrist to prevent the loss of the sword if it was dropped in combat.

Officers had a plaited leather sword-knot for the field but, for dress, Generals wore gold cord with an acorn end, other officers black and gold lace with a tassel. The scabbard was steel with two rings. The officer's sabre usually had a decorated hilt and blade, and the scabbard might be leather for officers below field grade, browned or bronzed steel for officers above and staff officers. Many officers had their own personal sabres, often very fancy imported European ones. Replacement cost to a trooper who lost his sabre was around $7.50.

Revolvers

The most widely used revolvers were the three already fully described in the Infantry book, the Colt Army ·44 M1860, Remington Army ·44 New Model and Starr Army ·44. These were top of the purchases made by the Federal Government between 1861 and 1866. Next in numbers were the Remington ·36 calibre M1861; Colt ·36 M1851; Savage ·36; Whitney ·36; Rogers and Spencer ·44; Colt ·36 M1861 and Pettingell ·44.

All of these revolvers were similar in performance and essential characteristics to the descriptions of the other three.

The revolver was carried in a holster of heavy black leather with a wide rounded flap, secured by a strap stitched under the flap which buttoned on to a brass stud on the holster. The holster was worn on the right, facing forward.

OVERLEAF: Union revolvers: (A) ·36 calibre Savage; (B) ·36 calibre Whitney; (C) ·44 calibre Rogers and Spencer; (D) ·40 calibre Deane and Adams; (E) ·44 calibre Pettingill.

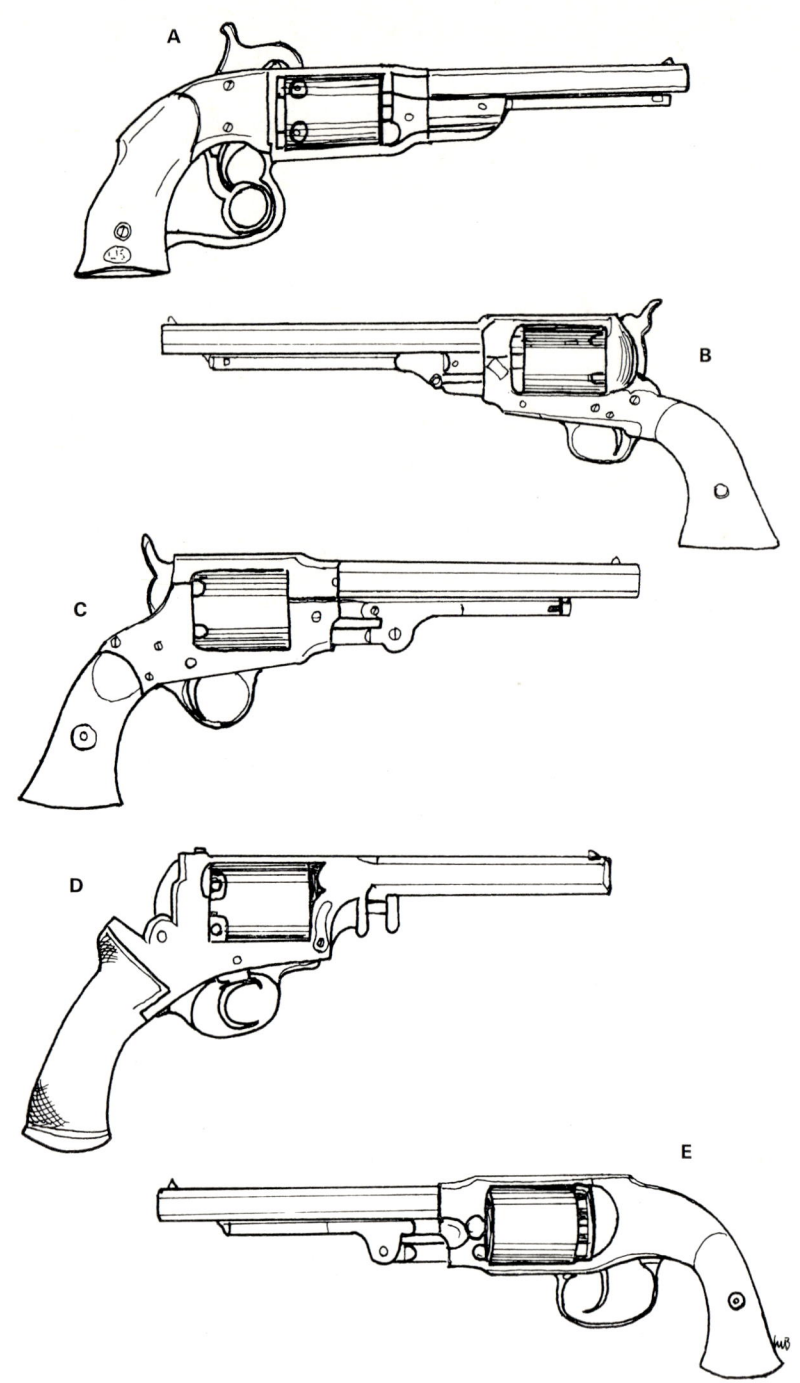

A

B

C

D

E

48

Carbines

A great variety of carbines were used, muzzle loaders, single-shot breech loaders and repeaters. Nineteen different types were actually purchased by the Federal authorities, eight or nine seeing the most use. Many of the other designs doubtless also saw action after private purchase. The most widely used are detailed below. Performance for all were much the same as the Sharps, except for the muzzle loaders which were much slower.

M1859 and M1863 Sharps Carbine

80,512 of these single-shot breech-loading single-action carbines were issued. The two models were essentially the same, ·52 and ·50 calibre respectively. Both had a rate of fire of eight rounds per minute with self-consuming linen cartridges; weight $7\frac{1}{4}$ lb; length $21\frac{1}{2}$-inch barrel, $37\frac{1}{2}$ inches overall. The breech block was dropped to open the chamber by levering the trigger guard down. Percussion was from disc primer or percussion caps. Early models were brass trimmed, later ones iron, with the barrel and sometimes the butt-plate blued, but frame, lock and barrel band case hardened in mottle colours; the stock was two-piece walnut, with a patch box on most M1859's but not on M1863's as a wartime economy measure. Sighted for 800 yards; effective range 500 yards; battle range 300 yards; 5-inch group at 100 yards.

One further variation was the special M1859 'Coffee Mill' Sharps, which had a coffee grinder with detachable crank in place of the big brass patch box, but not many were issued. For details see the illustration on page 46.

M1860, M1861, M1862 and M1864 Burnside Carbine

55,567 were purchased, most supplied by the Burnside Rifle Company; the designer being General A. Burnside. The carbine was ·54 calibre; length $39\frac{1}{2}$ inches overall, barrel 21 inches; and fired, by percussion cap, a perforated brass cartridge shaped almost like an ice-cream cone. The double trigger guard pressed together and was lowered to rotate the breech block and chamber into a vertical position to take the tapered case of the cartridge, the old cartridge being extracted by hand. Barrel was blued with lock-plate, trigger guard lever and all iron parts case hardened in mottle colours. The first two models had no forestocks.

Smith Percussion Breech-Loading Carbine

30,062 were purchased by the Federal Government. A single-shot ·50 calibre weapon it fired a paper-covered brass or rubber cartridge with flash holes in the end, by percussion cap; barrel $21\frac{5}{8}$ inches, 39 inches overall. To load, a T-shaped lifter in front of the trigger was pushed upwards which raised a spring catch on top of the barrel allowing the barrel to hinge down, opening the breech. Barrel, butt-plate, trigger guard and spring catch, blued; the remaining metal parts case hardened in mottle colours. Some carbines had sling swivels like infantry muskets instead of the normal sliding sling ring.

Starr Percussion Breech-Loading Carbine

Very similar to the Sharps, 25,603 were purchased. Single-shot ·54 calibre; 21-inch barrel, $37\frac{1}{2}$ inches overall; it fired a linen cartridge by percussion cap. The rear end of the trigger guard was unlatched and lowered to drop the breech block backwards to expose the chamber. Barrel was blued, the other

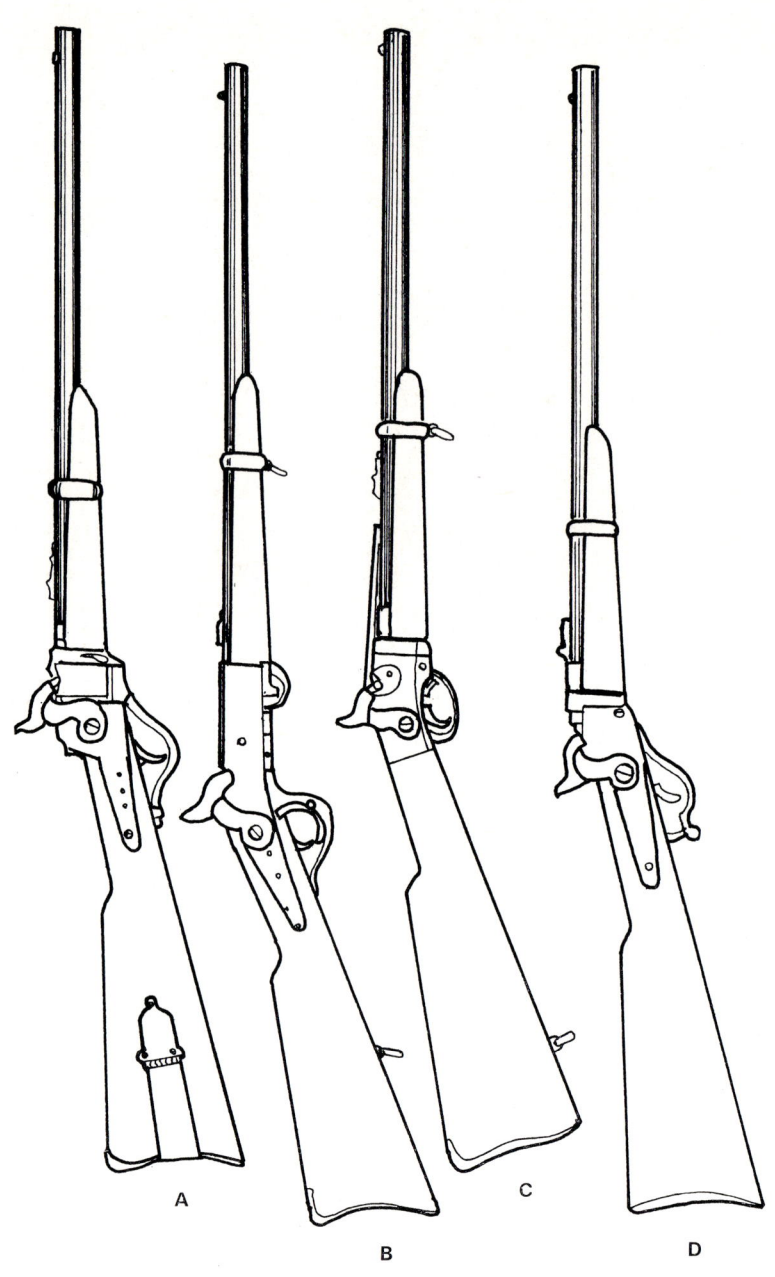

ABOVE: Union cavalry carbines: (A) Sharps carbine; (B) Burnside carbine; (C) Smith carbine; (D) Starr carbine.

metal parts case hardened in mottle colours. Manufactured by Starr Arms Company, makers of the Starr revolver.

Spencer Repeating Cartridge Carbine

Although it was not introduced until 1862 and was used in limited numbers until 1863, it was so popular that 94,196 were eventually provided. The ·52 calibre cartridge was rim-fire copper case, seven rounds being held in a tubular magazine held in the butt-stock, one in the chamber. The magazine was loaded into the butt through the butt-plate, the cartridges being fed into the breech by a coiled spring. The Spencer could also be fired as a single-shot carbine. Depressing and raising the trigger guard dropped the breech block, extracted the empty case, and moved a fresh cartridge into the chamber. The carbine had a 22-inch barrel, 39 inches overall. Only the barrel was blued, all other metal parts being case hardened. Rate of fire was ten rounds per minute. Sighted to 1,000 yards, effective range was 400 yards, battle range 2–300 yards, 6-inch group at 100 yards. Reloading rate using pre-loaded tubes was 10–12 seconds.

General George Armstrong Custer's Michigan Brigade, consisting of 1st, 5th, 6th and 7th Michigan Cavalry, drew 2,200 of the first Spencer carbines issued and soon became the backbone of Sheridan's cavalry. General James H. Wilson's force of 13,000 troopers, who raided so successfully deep into the South, were mainly armed with Spencers, to great effect.

Confederate

The Confederate cavalryman was armed like his Federal opponents with sabre, revolver and carbine, at least when supplies of all three were available. However, despite the problem of availability the Southern trooper almost completely abandoned the sabre after the first two years (sooner in the West) and carried two or more revolvers and the carbine, relying on their firepower in a charge. The more irregular units, like Mosbys, also preferred rifles or double-barrelled muzzle-loading shotguns to carbines; with often four revolvers, two in the belt and two in saddle holsters.

Sabres

The usual sabre carried was the light cavalry sabre, either the same Northern issue captured, or from stocks in the South at the outbreak of war, or a Confederate copy. It might also be an imported weapon from Europe, with curved blade and iron cup guard or long, straight blade and basket guard. The latter heavy style, around 38 inches long, was carried by Generals Wade Hampton and Nathan Bedford Forrest.

Revolvers

The situation with regard to revolvers was much the same. The main sources were captures from Union troops; pre-war weapons already in the South; revolvers made in the Confederacy, usually rather crude copies of the popular Northern guns; and imports from Europe, notably France and England.

The first two categories are covered by the details given under Union revolvers. The Southern manufactured weapons were of very varied quality and reliability, due mainly to the lack of materials and machinery. Brass was used a great deal for frames, for example for the Griswold and Grier (or Griswold and Gunnison) copy of the Colt Navy. Other makes included Leech and Rigdon,

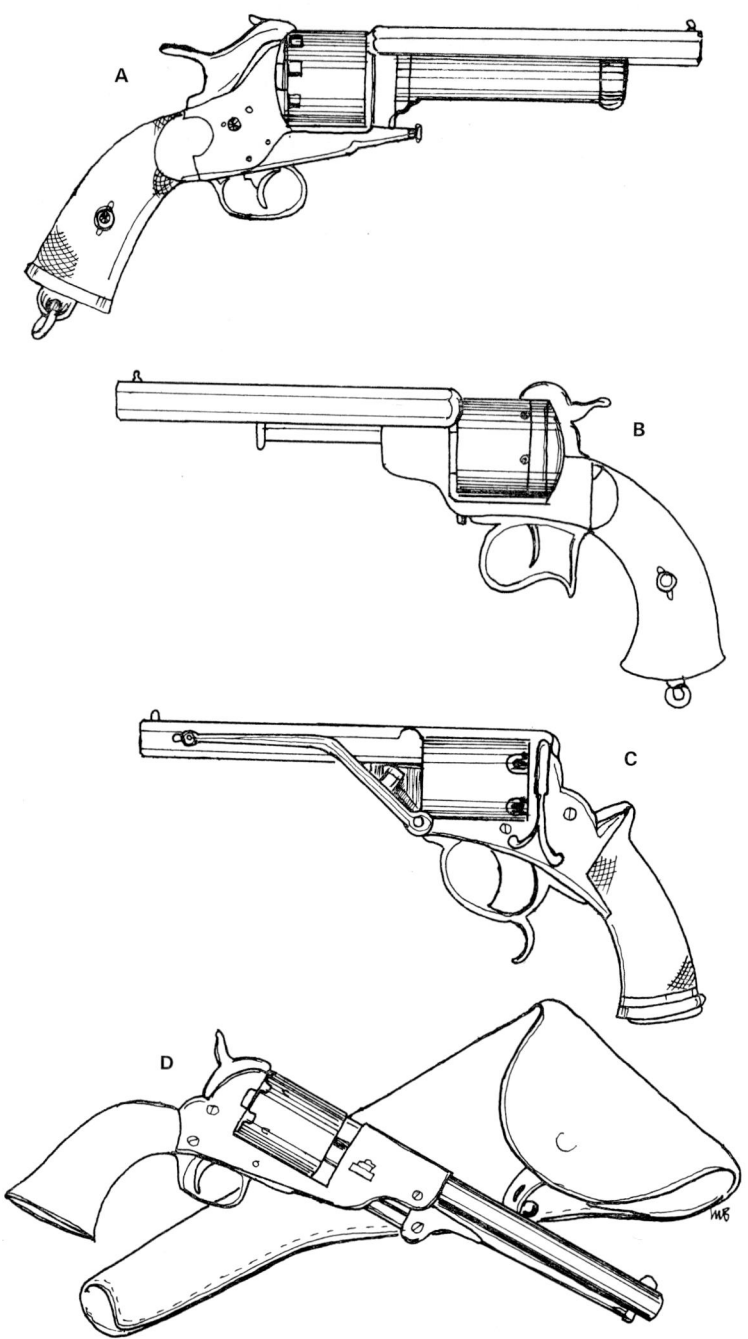

ABOVE: Confederate revolvers: (A) ·42 or ·36 calibre Le Mat; (B) ·42 Le Faucheaux; (C) ·36 or ·44 calibre Tranter; (D) ·44 or ·36 calibre Dance Bros copy of the Colt Dragoon with leather holster.

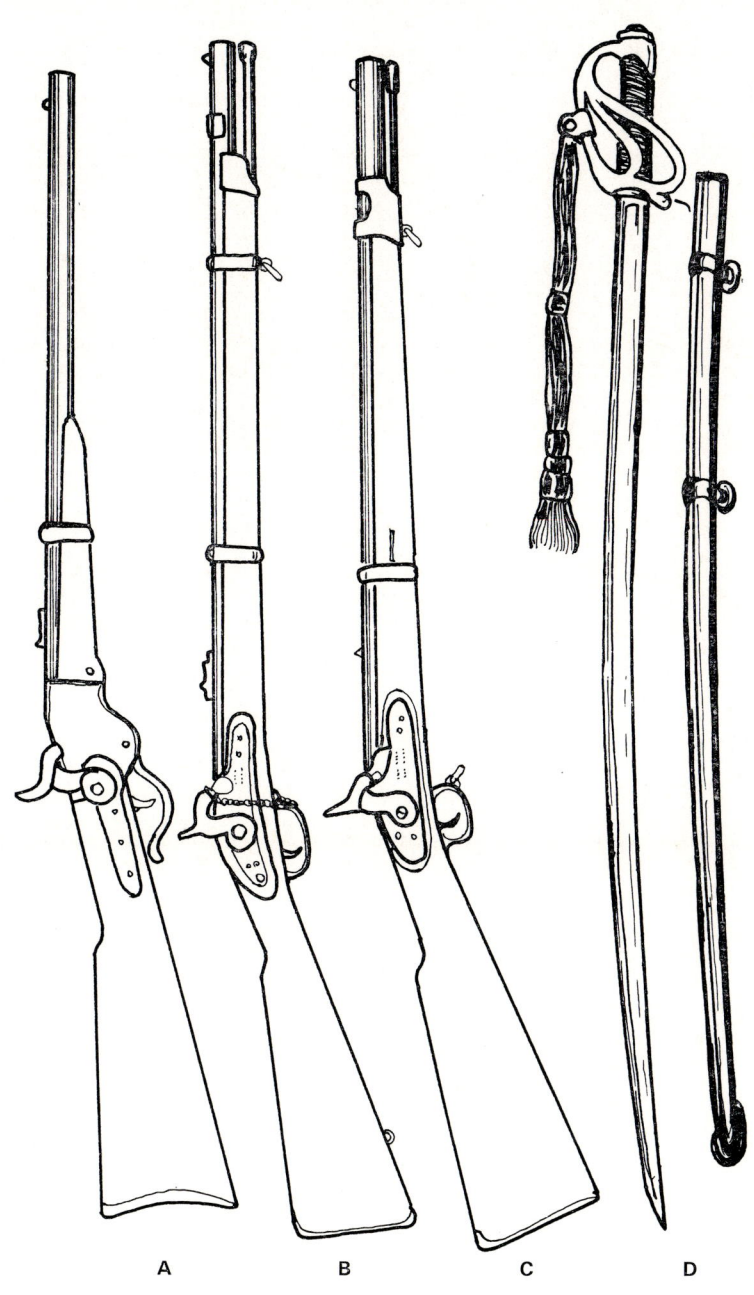

ABOVE: Confederate carbines and US pattern cavalry sabre: (A) Spencer repeating carbine; (B) Enfield Musketoon; (C) Murray carbine; (D) M1851 US cavalry sabre.

and Rigdon Ansley and Company (Colt Navy copies); J. H. Dance and Bros (Dragoon Colt ·44 and ·36 copies, with a peculiar flat frame and no recoil shield behind the cylinder); Spiller and Burr (Whitney copies); and Tucker and Sherrod (Dragoon Colt copies).

Imported weapons included the British Deane and Adams ·36 and ·44 calibre five-shot double-action, Tranter ·36 and ·44 calibre six-shot double-action revolvers; and the French Lefaucheaux pinfire in various calibres; the Le Mat 'Grapeshot' ·42 and ·36 calibre nine-shot cylinder with a ·63 calibre shotgun barrel below the main barrel, which could be fired by turning down the nose on the hammer. Some of these were actually made in America. Le Mats were carried by Generals P. G. T. Beauregard (once Le Mats partner), J. E. B. Stuart and P. Anderson.

Carbines

Again the remarks under the supply of sabres and revolvers applies equally well to the carbines used by the Confederate troopers.

The British Enfield single-shot muzzle-loading ·577 calibre was widely used by both sides at the beginning of the war, and Confederates preferred it because of its accuracy and rugged reliability. The ·58 calibre Minie ball and cartridge could be used. It followed the 'Tower' rifle musket pattern, and was some 40 inches long with two barrel bands and usually a strap sling.

Confederate manufactured guns included the Richmond carbine (contemporary reports say this was very unreliable and unpopular); J. P. Murrey muzzle-loading carbine; Cooke and Brother carbine (well liked, but muzzle loading and therefore slow); a Richmond copy of the Sharps breech loader (some were good, others very unreliable). A small number of Morse single-shot cartridge breech-loading carbines were produced. The metal cartridges could only be fired one at a time, but the carbine had a Winchester style trigger guard which was, in fact, immovable, and presumably served for show only!

BELOW: Different types of cartridge and priming used in revolvers and carbines:
(A) Pinfire cartridge; (B) Burnside cartridge; (C) Sharps paper cartridge; (D) Sharps linen cartridge; (E) Percussion caps; (F) Maynard tape primer.

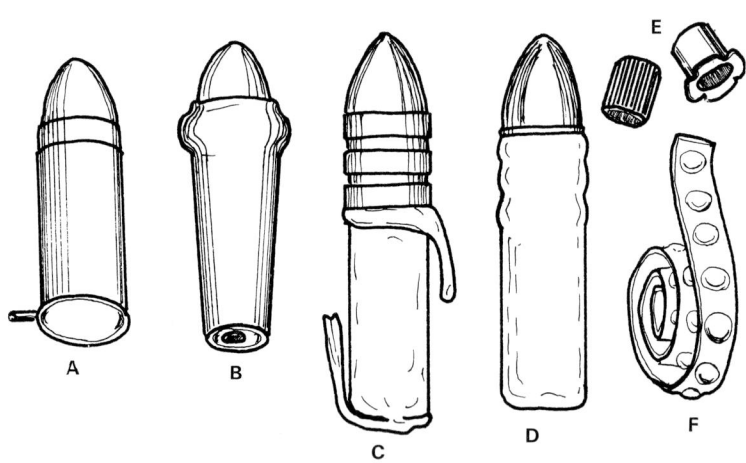

Chapter 6: Indians

Organization

BOTH sides raised Indian regiments; at least 5,500 redskin cavalrymen were recruited by the Confederacy, and around 4,000 served in the Union infantry. The South recruited Indians much earlier than the North, promising the creation of an all-Indian nation in what is now Oklahoma. Many of the Indian tribes in this area were originally Southern, owning negro slaves, and had been deported West by the Federal Government with an escort of the army now fighting the Confederacy. Leading figure in the raising of Southern Indian units was Brigadier-General Albert Pike, a white man who was made commander of the Confederate Department of Indian Territory. He formed the Indians into regiments and battalions on tribal lines.

The official records list the following Confederate Indian units.

1st Cherokee Cavalry

1st Cherokee Regiment

2nd Cherokee Mounted Rifles (Colonel Stand Watie, three-quarters Cherokee and later to be Brigadier-General, and one of the last Confederates to surrender on June 23, 1865. The men were mostly half-breeds).

Drews Cherokee Mounted Rifles (1st Cherokee Mounted Rifles; Colonel John Drew; nearly all full bloods).

Holts Cherokee Battalion

1st Chickasaw Cavalry Battalion

1st Chickasaw Regiment

Pickens Chickasaw Battalion

1st Choctaw Battalion

1st Choctaw Cavalry Regiment

1st Choctaw Cavalry War Regiment (In 1864, the 2nd Choctaw Cavalry Regiment)

3rd Choctaw Regiment

1st Chocsaw and Chickasaw Mounted Rifles (Colonel Douglas H. Cooper)

1st Creek Cavalry Battalion

1st Creek Regiment (1st Creek Regiment Mounted Volunteers; Colonel D. N. McIntosh, who was part Scots, part Creek)

2nd Creek Regiments (2nd Creek Regiment Mounted Volunteers; Lieutenant-Colonel C. McIntosh, brother of the 1st's commander)

Kenards Creek Squadron

McSmiths Creek Company

Osage Battalion (Major Broke Arm)

1st Seminole Cavalry Battalion (Lieutenant-Colonel John Jumper)

Except for Pike and Cooper all officers were Indian or part Indian. Some Cherokees in the Carolinas served as Scouts for the Confederates in the South-east.

INDIAN TROOPS

The figure on the left is a Confederate Indian trooper wearing a fringed Indian shirt which could have been any shade of brown, and wrap-around legging trousers with the distinctive triangular shaped flap at the bottom. Equipment consisted of a flap-over holster, on a low-slung belt, to hold the favoured revolver, and a large knife carried in a sheath (not visible) in the trouser belt. The hair is worn long and loose in Indian style. Feathers in the head band were for Indians only, but feathers in hats were often worn by white troopers.

On the right is a Corporal of a Union Indian regiment, wearing the regulation kepi, fatigue blouse and trousers with cap box and waist belt. Non-regulation items were the knife in a beaded and fringed sheath, head band and moccasins. The blanket roll is an indication of the poor equipment issued to the Indians, in this case replacing the knapsack and cross belt, etc. The kepi has no infantry insignia—indeed, these were probably not issued. The musket is an old M1855 Harpers Ferry but might even have been a M1812 Flintlock.

In the official Confederate report of September 30, 1864 on the Army of the Trans-Mississippi Department, the Indian Cavalry Division under Brigadier-General Douglas H. Cooper was organised in two brigades.

1st Indian Brigade, General Stand Watie

1st Cherokee (Colonel Robert C. Parks)
2nd Cherokee (Colonel Wm. P. Adair)
Cherokee Battalion (Major Joseph A Scales)
1st Creek (Colonel Daniel N McIntosh)
2nd Creek (Colonel Chilly McIntosh)
Creek Squadron (Captain R Kenard)
1st Osage Battalion (Major Broken Arm)
1st Seminole Battalion (Lieutenant-Colonel John Jumper)

2nd Indian Brigade, Colonel Tandy Walker

1st Chickasaw Battalion (Lieutenant-Colonel Lemuel M. Reynolds)
1st Choctaw Battalion (Lieutenant-Colonel Jackson McCurtain)
1st Choctaw and Chickasaw Battalion (Lieutenant-Colonel James Riley)
2nd Choctaw (Colonel Simpson N. Folsom)
Reserve Squadron (Captain George Washington)

In addition to these two brigades there were two unattached white units, the 1st Battalion Texas Sharpshooters (Major James Burnet) and the 20th Texas (Major John R Johnson).

Artillery support for fhe Indian Division comprised the 7th Mounted Artillery Battalion (Captain W. Butler Krumbhaar), consisting Dashiells Battery (Captain George R. Dashiell), Krumbhaars Battery (Lieutenant W. M. Stafford) and Howells Battery (Captain Sylvanus Howell), all Texan units.

The Federal authorities eventually agreed to Indian regiments being recruited, although Secretary-of-War Edwin M. Stanton's ban had, in fact, been already broken. An entire company of the 53rd New York Infantry—D'Epinenils Zouaves—was made up of Tuscarora Indians. Eventually in 1862 three regiments of infantry were recruited, the 1st (mostly Creeks), 2nd and 3rd Indian Regiments, and were designated Home Guard. Many were Cherokees, Creeks and Osages. They were brigaded with Kansas Cavalry and Artillery and soon sent South to what is now Northern Oklahoma. The Seneca raised a company who served in a New York regiment, and a band of Delawares scouted for the Federal Army in the Mississippi Valley area. One Indian unit served as Sharpshooters in the second battle of Fredericksburg, but these may have been the Seneca Company. The Colonel and some of the field and line officers were white, but most of the Captains of companies were Indians. Colonel William A. Phillips commanded the Indian Brigade.

Promises made by the white authorities or the Indians were not very often kept. The Indians' service throughout the war was a confusion of military red tape, white prejudice, and tribal jealousies and intrigue. The opposing Governments never fulfilled their promises, and many braves switched sides again and again to join whichever army offered most, or had won the last battle. However, the official records show that just as Confederate Indians were amongst the last to surrender, 1,018 Union Indians of those who served died for the Union.

Tactics and Weapons

Brigadier-General Pike, and apparently other expert Indian leaders, allowed the Indians to fight their own way. The Confederates were mounted on wiry

Plains ponies, which were sometimes tethered to the rear whilst the braves fought as infantry. However they did operate as cavalry, especially after the collapse of the Confederate strength west of the Mississippi, when warfare degenerated into a series of raids. It was in this role of irregular cavalry that the redskins came into their own, and Stand Watie, now the Indians' leader after Pike had resigned, and John Ross principal chief of the Cherokees had deserted to the Union, harassed Federal supply trains. In one surprise attack he even captured a U.S. supply ship on the Arkansas River!

The usual weapons were carried, except the sabre, and the Confederate Indians favourite weapon was the shotgun, widely used by the Rebels. By special authority at least Colonel Drew's Cherokee full bloods had bows and arrows, tomahawks and scalping knives. Lances and spears also appear to have been used. The Union Indians asked for, but were refused, 'wagons that shoot', ie, artillery, and were issued very poor quality muskets at the start.

The Indians fought in a number of battles, but only met face to face in a few. The first such clash was Locust Grove, in which the Federal redskins with white troops defeated a similarly mixed Confederate force. Near Newtonia, in a fight for the Granby lead mines, Colonel Cooper's Choctaws and Chickasaws defeated Colonel W. A. Phillips' Federal Cherokees, and scalps were taken, as they were reported to have been at the earlier Pea Ridge. At Pea Ridge some 3,500 Confederate braves fought as a Brigade, forming over a fifth of the Rebel force. The Confederates were defeated and Stand Watie's men covered the retreat. There were no Indians in the Union force.

Uniforms

No special uniform appears to have been authorized for Indian units on either side. The 53rd New York wore a Zouave style uniform with tasselled red fezzes and the usual baggy Zouave trousers. The other Union regiments appear to have worn the regulation uniform, whilst retaining their traditional hair styles. A contemporary account describes the small kepis perched on their full heads of hair as comical and ludicrous.

The Confederate units wore the same style of uniforms as the other cavalry. Stand Watie's Cherokee Mounted Rifles (Plate 5) wore grey shirts or jackets with yellow collar and cuffs. Trousers also appear to have been grey with the usual stripe for NCOs. The hat or kepi usually had the traditional feather. A decorated breech cloth was worn, fringed buckskin leggings and moccasins, and the headband. Knives were carried in beaded and decorated fringed sheaths. Braves often stripped before going into battle, wearing only trousers or breech cloth, leggings and moccasins. Undoubtedly, as the war progressed and shortages grew more acute, the Indians became more and more indistinguishable from civilian Indians and the other Rebel troopers.

Chapter 7: Machine-guns

FEW people realize that machine-guns were, in fact, used in the Civil War. The guns used can be divided into two groups, true machine-guns, ie, continuous rapid fire, and volley guns. The latter were mainly employed in defence, particularly of bridges, and indeed became known as 'covered bridge guns'.

Of the true machine-guns only three saw action, the Confederate Williams Machine-gun, the Union Agar or Union Repeating Gun, and the Union Gatling Gun. It was the latter which went on to win fame in later models, but oddly enough which played the smallest part in the Civil War. Volley guns used in the conflict were usually either the Vandenberg Volley Gun or the Billinghurst and Requa Battery Gun M1862. Only those guns which were used in anger are dealt with and anyone interested in other models, such as the Ripley which never went into production, will find information in the books quoted as sources in the Bibliography.

Williams Machine-gun: 1-pounder, 1 barrel, 1·25 to 1·57 calibre

This Confederate 'secret weapon' was invented by Captain Williams of Covington, Kentucky. The single barrel was 4 feet long, made of iron, and mounted on a light one-horse double-shafted mountain howitzer-type carriage. Rate of fire was 60–65 rounds per minute, with a range of up to 2,000 yards. The piece was manned by a crew of three. One fed self-consuming paper cartridges into the breech from above by hand. The second placed percussion caps on to a nipple on the left-hand side of the chamber, under an automatic hammer synchronized to the breech mechanism. The third cranked the handle on the right side which closed and locked the breech block and dropped the hammer on the cap. As the block slid back the hammer rose clear of the nipple on a cam. A 1-lb shell or 'bolt', or a king-size load of buckshot wrapped in paper, could be fired. The buckshot acted like a gigantic shotgun at close range, and was extremely lethal! These guns saw extensive service throughout the war.

After testing, the first model was used by Picketts' Brigade at Fair Oaks on May 31, 1862, where it was reported as having 'killed Federals so fast they never knew what hit them'. The Confederate Government ordered 42 guns to make seven batteries of six guns each. The guns were made at Lynchburg and Richmond, Virginia, and Mobile, Alabama. In 1863 at Blue Springs a battery with the 4th Kentucky Cavalry shot up a detachment of the 7th Ohio Cavalry. Several guns under Captain Williams' command served with Picketts' Brigade.

Unfortunately the gun had its drawbacks. When it was fired for any length of time the breech expanded from the heat and failed to seat properly. The South's acute shortage of high-grade steel meant that the problem of overheating could not be overcome successfully, and this fact seems to have kept the Williams Gun from attaining more prominence. Despite its failings it was rated very reliable.

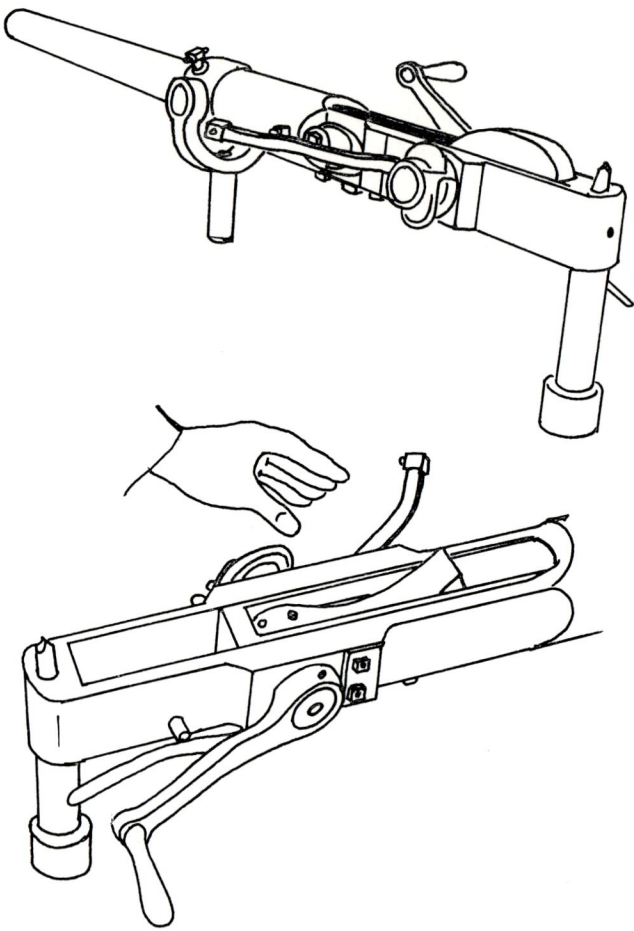

ABOVE: Confederate Williams machine-gun: (A) Breech open for loading; (B) Breech closed ready to fire, hand shown to indicate size of breech.

Agar Machine-gun: 0·58 calibre, single-barrelled

This gun was also known as the 'Coffee Mill' gun because the cartridges were fed down a hopper shaped like an old-fashioned coffee grinder. Officially it was the Union Repeating Gun. The manufacturers described it as 'an army in 6 feet square'.

The rate of fire was 120 rounds per minute. The gun was mounted on a two-wheeled carriage similar to that of the normal artillery piece, except that two equipment boxes were fixed one on either side of the axle. In order to reduce the danger of overheating of the barrel two spares were carried. Steel containers holding combustible cartridges, or loose powder and ball (75 grains), and with the nipple for the cap at the end, were loaded into the hopper and were gravity-fed into a recess at the back of the barrel. Containers, which also acted as firing chambers, were pushed forward to form prolongations of the barrel by action of the crank and were locked by a rising wedge. As the crank was turned the cam-operated hammer fell on the percussion cap.

BELOW: Union Agar machine-gun shown with and without shield. Note the hopper for the ammunition which gave it its nickname of the 'Coffee Mill' gun, not to be confused with the weapon on page 46 which was for grinding coffee.

Further turning of the handle released the wedge, a lever pushed the empty container out of the recess, and a fresh one dropped into place. A small shield could be fitted in front of the hopper to protect it and the operator from enemy fire.

The gun was only adopted under protest by the Union Army on Lincoln's personal intervention, and ten pieces were purchased late in 1861 for $1,300 each—twice the estimated cost of their manufacture. Two guns were with Colonel J. W. Geary's 28th Pennsylvania Volunteers on March 29, 1862, at Middleburg, Virginia, on the Potomac, where they 'cut to pieces' and routed two squadrons of Confederate Cavalry at 800 yards. Despite this Geary returned them to Washington with a report that they were 'inefficient and unsafe to operate'. In June 1862, North Carolina Infantry under Brigadier-General I. Trimble, CSA, captured two 'revolving cannon with hoppers into which bullets were poured', and reported that the devilish Yankee contraptions had blazed away for two hours before anyone could get near them. Two of these guns were used during the seige of Petersburg.

The mechanical unreliability and weight of these pieces, together with the problem of ammunition supply (problems which, in fact, applied to all the machine-guns of the period), eventually resulted in the guns being relegated to covered bridge defence along with the volley guns. In August 1865 Agar guns were sold at an army surplus sale at Fort Monroe for $5–8 each!

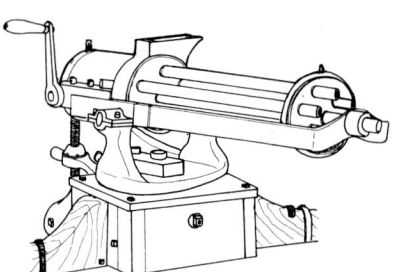

Gatling gun in close-up showing breech and muzzle detail.

Gatling Machine-gun: 0·58 calibre, 6 barrels

The first Gatling gun was designed by Dr Richard J. Gatling in 1861, as a special weapon to defend buildings, causeways and bridges. In 1862 Gatling demonstrated his first working model, which was fundamentally the Agar principle improved by the multi-barrelled arrangement of the Ripley gun. The gun had six barrels equally spaced around a central shaft, which were revolved by a crank. Each barrel had its own bolt, and cocking and firing were performed by cam action through a gear drive arrangement. Rate of fire, in a prime performance, was 250 rounds per minute. The M1862 Type II used copper rim-fire in place of the paper cartridges and percussion cap originally used. Both models were loaded by gravity feed from a hopper and were mounted on carriages like those of the normal artillery piece.

The U.S. Ordnance was not interested in Gatling's invention, however, and would not order any. Eventually, in 1864, General Butler bought twelve after a field demonstration and used them very effectively at Petersburg. The taper of the bores, necessary because barrels and chambers did not always align exactly, impaired velocity and accuracy. The greatly improved model of 1865 came too late for the war.

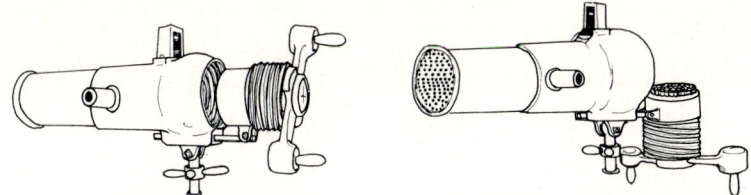

Vandenberg Volley-gun: Various calibres, 85 to 451 barrels

General O. Vendenberg designed a new system of 'artillery' using up to 451 barrel clusters firing musket balls in unison, but his idea met with only limited success.

A screw-type breech held cartridges in individual chambers and slid into a key-way. Copper sleeves were forced into a counter-bored chamber for a gas-tight seal when the breech was screwed into the rear of the barrels. A centre charge fired by a percussion cap set off a whole volley; or sections of barrels could be blocked off and fired separately. In tests, a 191-barrel model put 90 per cent in a 6-foot square at 100 yards. Recoil was very strong, and this and its considerable weight made the weapon of limited use. A carriage like that of the normal artillery piece was used

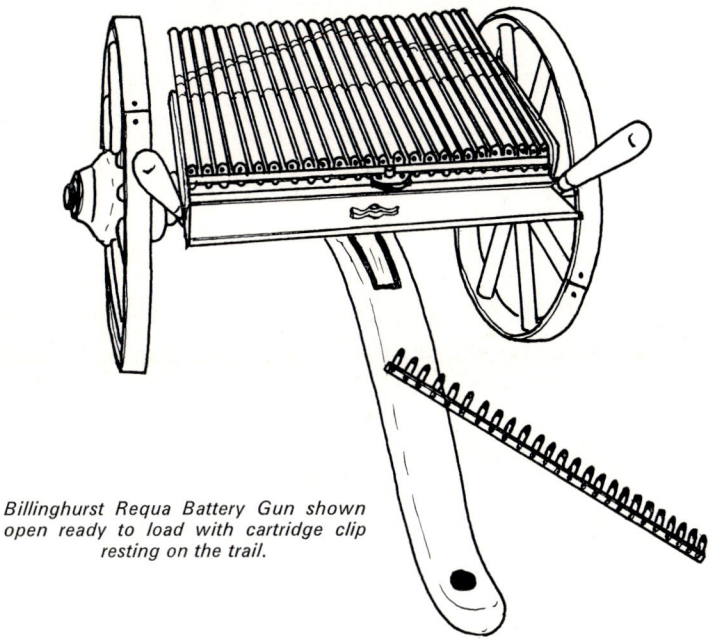

Billinghurst Requa Battery Gun shown open ready to load with cartridge clip resting on the trail.

Billinghurst Requa Battery Gun: 0·58 calibre, 25 barrels

Built late in 1861 by the Billinghurst Company of Rochester, New York, this gun had 25 barrels mounted flat on a light metal platform on a two-wheel carriage. The sliding breech was operated by a lever and the barrels were loaded by light steel cartridges with an ignition hole in the oval base held in special clips for quick loading. When the gun was loaded, a channel behind the cartridges was filled with powder, which was ignited by a percussion cap struck by a hammer firing all barrels simultaneously. The barrels could be moved laterally for 'spread'. Paper cartridges were not inserted in the steel cases, but each case was loaded by hand with loose powder, and a patched ball was used in the belief that it gave greater accuracy. With a crew of three, seven volleys per minute could be fired. The exposure of the powder to rain and stray sparks was, however, a distinct disadvantage. Effective range was in excess of 1,000 yards.

Select Bibliography

Albaugh II, W. A. and Simmons, E. N., *Confederate Arms*, Stackpole 1957.

American Rifleman, *Civil War Small Arms*, NRA 1959.

Coggins, J., *Arms and Equipment of the Civil War*, Doubleday 1962.

Confederate Historical Society, *Uniforms of the Confederacy*.

Cunningham, F., *General Stand Watie's Confederate Indians*, Naylor.

Dyer, F. H., *A Compendium of the War of Rebellion compiled and arranged from the Official Records of the Federal and Confederate Armies, 1908*.

Foster-Harris, *The Look of the Old West*, Bonanza.

Halsey Jr, A., *Who Fired the First Shot ?*, Hawthorn.

Milhollen, H. D., *Horsemen Blue and Grey*, Oxford, N.Y.

Military Collector and Historian, *Journal of the Company of Military Historians*, Washington DC.

Miller, F. T. and Larrier, R. S., Editors, *The Photographic History of the Civil War*, 10 Volumes, Review of Reviews 1911.

Pakula, M. H., *Centennial Album of the Civil War*, Yoseloff 1960.

Patton Museum Society, *The United States Cavalry*, Publication No 2.

Rodenbough, T. F., *The Photographic History of the Union and Confederate Cavalry in the Civil War (1861-1865)*, Benchmark.

Smith, W. H. B., *Small Arms of the World*, Stackpole.

Tancig, W. J., *Confederate Military Land Units*, Yoseloff.

Todd, F. P., *Soldiers of the American Army 1775-1954*, Regnery.

Wahl, P. and Toppel, D., *The Gatling Gun*, Avco, NY.